GULZAR'S
Aandhi

Saba Mahmood Bashir is a poet, author and a translator. Her first book was a collection of poems, *Memory Past* (2006) brought out by Writers' Workshop. She has also authored *I Swallowed the Moon: The Poetry of Gulzar* (HarperCollins India, 2013) and translated Gulzar's screenplays of Premchand's *Godaan* and *Nirmala and Other Stories*. Her forthcoming book is a translation of selected short stories by Manto.

GULZAR'S
Aandhi

INSIGHTS INTO THE FILM

SABA MAHMOOD BASHIR

HarperCollins *Publishers* India

First published in India by
HarperCollins *Publishers* in 2019
A-75, Sector 57, Noida, Uttar Pradesh 201301, India
www.harpercollins.co.in

2 4 6 8 10 9 7 5 3 1

P-ISBN: 978-93-5302-508-3
E-ISBN: 978-93-5302-509-0

Typeset in 11.5/15 Bembo at
Manipal Digital Systems, Manipal

Printed and bound at
Thomson Press (India) Ltd

For Amir and Sana

Contents

જી

Preface

Cinema in India, as elsewhere too, is one of the most crucial parameters to gauge the changing shifts in society – at political, sociocultural and even economic levels. A film is not created in a vacuum. It has its own distinct space, roots and character.

At the outset, I wish to declare that I believe in looking at Hindustani cinema based on Indian parameters. Cinema in India is a genre in itself. One should not look at and analyse it on parameters made commonplace by the West. The Western definitions of the words 'musical' and 'melodrama' are not applicable to Indian cinema. In the same way, the idea of a 'multi-starrer' or a 'devotional' film might sound alien in world cinema.

When a film is made *for* Indian audiences, it needs to be evaluated and understood from *their* perspective. The perspective of looking at a film should depend on the origins and circumstances of its viewers. I am not sure if I subscribe to Paul Willemen's 'Cinephilia', the theory which suffers from considerable neglect in film theory.[1] Instead I consciously attempt to look at Indian films through a certain innate Indian-ness.

That said, I have translated Gulzar's *Aandhi* on self-established paradigms. An attempt has been made to look at the structure of the film, by being cognizant of the fact that the story is set against the turbulent political backdrop of elections and politicking between various political parties and its leaders. The analysis of the cinematic text led to the exploration of the visual, narrative and self-reflexive elements of the film. This book further explores the very essence of the film: the love story between a hotel manager (JK), and his ambitious wife (Aarti), who aspires to be a minister one day. A close textual analysis has been adopted to view the film and delve into its layers.

Sumita S. Chakravarty[2] points out that the Hindi-Urdu word for a film screen is 'purdah', or curtain – that which

---

1 Lalita Gopalan, in the essay 'Hum Aapke Hain Kaun? – Cinephilia and Indian Films' in *Asian Cinemas: A Reader and Guide* (ed. Dimitris Eleftheriotis and Gary Needham, Edinburgh: Edinburgh University Press, 2006), quotes Paul Willemen and his take on Cinephillia; see p. 326.

2 S. Chakravarty, *National Identity in Indian Popular Cinema 1947–87*, Austin: Austin University of Texas Press, 1993, p. 32.

hides rather than reveals. Popular Indian conception of the cinema, therefore, associates film with the invisible rather than the visible. Building on this premise, one can unravel the ambiguity apparent in a film.

I am also wary of the generic classification of films into 'art' cinema and 'popular' cinema. These parameters have been created by different theorists and critics. However, most films cannot fall in such distinct categories. What are the base parameters that put the films in tight compartments? Would a film be 'art' if it depicted the harsh reality of a country? If it featured a romance-driven plot with song and dance sequences, would it be 'commercial' cinema? It doesn't stop there. There are various categories in commercial cinema as well – mythological, historical, action, romantic-comedy, etc. Also, there are Indian commercial films which do well overseas, and has an international presence. What about films like *Pyaasa* (1957), *Mother India* (1957) and *Mughal-e-Azam* (1960) – to name only a few – where the so-called boundaries between art and commercial cinema clearly seem to have blurred and merged? *Aandhi* is one such film. It was a commercial success – featuring a strong, memorable love story, which was also a tongue-in-cheek comment on the then political scenario of the country.

This book is divided into five chapters. It begins by looking at its filmmaker, Gulzar, and how *Aandhi* is a director's film, all the way. The first chapter also focusses on why he chose this story, originally written by Kamleshwar.

The second chapter focusses on the controversy surrounding the film. Critics pointed out the resemblance of the film's female protagonist, Suchitra Sen, to the then prime minister of India, Indira Gandhi. This eventually led to a ban on the screening of the film. It also expands on how *Aandhi* goes beyond a mere romantic film and becomes not only a statement of the then political situation in India, but also alludes to the undercurrents between the common man and his ideas about the political leadership of the country.

The next chapter is on the film's stellar cast – comprising not only the actors who played the two protagonists but also those in supporting roles, all well etched out.

Poetry plays a crucial role in the screenplay; so the fourth chapter is on the songs, which played a major part in making the film a commercial success. Three of the songs in the film showcase three different stages in the life of the couple and their complex relationship. Another important song, a qawwali, is a strong political commentary on how a common man views politicians.

The last chapter in the book looks at the language used in the film. The dialogues have both wit and humour – both in scenes involving the personal lives of the couple and those highlighting the political drama.

PREFACE

The interview of the filmmaker has been referenced throughout the book. It has also been provided as an appendix, as it gives a strong insight into the many things that went into the making of *Aandhi*. The lyrics of the songs form the other appendix.

chapter one

The Auteur

CR

Toot ki skaakh pe baitha koi
bunta hai resham ke taage
lamha lamha khol raha hai
patta patta been raha hai
ek-ek saans baja kar sunta hai saudayee
ek-ek saans ko kholke apne tan pe liptata jaata hai

apni hee saanson ka qaidi
resham ka shaayar ek din
apne hee tagon mein ghutkar mar jayega[3]

(Sitting on a mulberry branch
Weaves some silk threads

---

3 Gulzar, 'Portrait of a Poet', *Pukhraj*, New Delhi: Rupa, 2005, p. 167.

Unwrapping each moment
Picking each leaf
Listening to every breath
Drapes self with each breath

Prisoner of his own breath
This poet of silk
Will die smothered in his own threads)

Gulzar. The name says it all. The poet, who is also a lyricist, filmmaker and dialogue writer, has more layers to his persona that one can delve into. Author of several anthologies of poems (*Kuch Aur Nazmein, Pukhraj, Raat Pashmine Ki, Triveni, Yaar Julahe* and *Pandra Paanch Pachchatar*) and writer of short stories (*Raavi Paar, Aththaniyan*), he has not only written extensively for children (*Bosky ka Panchantantra 1–5, Karadi Tales, Potli Baba ki, Mangoo aur Mangli, Bosky ke Taal Pataal, Hindi for Heart* and many more), but has also been translating from Bengali, Marathi and English.

Gulzar's mass appeal, however, is through cinema. Writing for Hindustani cinema for more than half a century, Gulzar started his career with assisting filmmaker Bimal Roy for *Kabuliwala* (1961). Based on a short story of the same name by Rabindranath Tagore, it was for this film that he also wrote the song '*Ganga aaye kahan se*' (Ganga, where do you come from?). However, the song that got released first was from the film *Bandini* (1962); based on

Vaishnavite poetry, the lyrics went: '*Mora gora ang lei le, mohe shyam rang dei de*' (Take away my fair colour, give me the colour of Krishna). Gulzar calls this song his 'entry pass' into cinema. Although he was noticed with his very first song, it was with '*Humne dekhi hai in aankhon ki mehakti khushboo*' (I have seen the fragrance in these eyes) from *Khamoshi* (1969) that he truly arrived. On the one hand he was applauded for the use of his unusual and juxtaposed imagery – which later became his signature style – and on the other, he was also criticized by traditional poets for this approach. Whatever the argument may have been, it was this song that brought Gulzar to the forefront of poetry writing in cinema.

Born in Deena (now in Pakistan) in 1934, Gulzar had witnessed the Partition from close quarters. It was amidst that turmoil that he crossed the border and came to Delhi, where he settled initially, before moving to Bombay. In his early days there, he worked at a garage, trying to fend for himself. But destiny had something else in store for him. After working in the garage for about seven years[4], he found himself at the studio where Bimal Roy was at work and got his first break as his assistant. When someone gets trained under the adept directorship of someone like Bimal Roy, what else can one expect to imbibe but exceptional directorial skills? In Gulzar's case, it was coupled with his poetic craft and a love of words.

---

4   M. Gulzar, *because he is…*, New Delhi: Rupa, 2004, p. 23.

A unique characteristic that distinguishes Gulzar the filmmaker, is that when he is at the helm, he goes beyond being just the director. He also writes the screenplay, dialogues and lyrics, taking full ownership of the film and makes it distinctly different from the work of other filmmakers. Viewers can notice his signature style in every frame. In over hundred years of Hindustani cinema, there have been only a handful of other filmmakers who have donned all these hats.

Gulzar's journey as a film poet

Gulzar has experimented with several genres while penning poetry for cinema. It would not be wrong to say that he is the only poet in the industry who has such a versatile repertoire of work. Apart from his love songs, he has written political satires, hymns and prayers, songs for children – based on folklore and legends – and even philosophical ones. To sum up his songwriting in a brief category is being unjust to his oeuvre, but here are some of his more popular ones, categorized according to genres.

Love songs

Love and romance are perhaps the most popular themes in Hindustani cinema. It is, therefore, no surprise that most poets working in the industry have many love songs in their body of work. Gulzar is no exception to this: he has an enviable legacy of love songs. But what makes his work different from other lyricists, is his treatment of language and his use of imagery, both of which have a distinct and unique touch.

Just living the essence of love is apparent in *Anubhav*'s (1971) '*Meri jaan mujhe jaan na kaho*' (My dear, don't call me a dear) where a lover tells her partner not to call her by endearing names. Simple as the words may sound, they strike a chord with listeners and the underlying essence comes through. '*Maine tere liye saat rang ke sapne bune*' (I've woven dreams of seven colours for you) from *Anand* (1971) reminds one of the pure and pristine love a lover bestows on his/her beloved. '*Ek hasin nigah ka dil pe saaya hai*' (A beauty has cast its shadow on me) from *Maya Memsaab* (1993) communicates the inexplicable feeling of being in love in such a simplified verse. Another gem from the same film, '*Iss dil mein bas kar dekho to*' (If you came and lived once in my heart) beckons the lover to come and love her.

If there is contentment and happiness in '*Tum aa gaye ho, noor aa gaya hai*' (Your presence has brought light in my life) from *Aandhi* (1975) there are feelings of exuberance as expressed in '*Aaj kal paon zameen par nahin padte*' (These days, I feel no ground beneath the feet) in *Ghar* (1977). '*Do dewane ek shahar mein*' from *Gharonda* (1978) celebrates togetherness, and nothing more. Such companionship is also revealed in '*Tu mere paas hai*' (You are with me) from *Satya* (1998). The unreleased film *Libaas* (1993) had two melodious songs, '*Seeli hawa choo gayee*' (The damp breeze touched me) and '*Khamosh sa afsana*' (The silent tale) which express love of the silent, unexpressed kind. Another song which indicates a quiet love which only Nature (the earth and the sky) is witness to, is '*Chup chup ke, chori se*' (Quietly, silently…) from *Bunty aur Babli* (2005).

The naughtiness of a lover is aptly described in '*Dil to bachcha hai jee*' (My heart is childlike) from *Ishqiya* (2010) where an elderly man is helplessly smitten by a woman much younger than him. '*Dheere jalna*' (Smoulder slowly) from *Paheli* (2005) tries to capture the intimacy between lovers. The chartbuster '*Chaiyya chaiyya*' from *Dil Se* (1998) takes love to another level altogether, transcending the boundaries of earthly love and spirituality, where the lover believes that if one is in love, paradise lies beneath their feet and compares his beloved to the *kalma* (the line which marks the acceptance of the Islamic faith) and wishes to keep her safe like a *taveez* (amulet).

The pining lover from Gulzar's poetry leaves an everlasting impression on the hearts of listeners. If '*Tum pukar lo*' (If only you would call) from *Khamoshi* (1969) beautifully captures the pathos of the lover and cries out for being remembered, '*Koi hota jisko apna kehte*' (Wishing for someone I could call my own) from *Mere Apne* (1971) is about the desire to be loved by someone. Again, the song '*Jab bhi yeh dil udaas hota hai*' (Every time this heart is sad) from *Seema* (1971) follows the same trajectory with as much intensity as the song '*Tere bina jiya jaye na*' (Can't live without you) from *Ghar* (1977). Another song about remembering the loved one is '*Yaara seeli seeli, birah ki raat ka jalna*' (Oh the dampening embers of the night of parting) from *Lekin* (1990); the song '*Tum gaye, sab gaya*' (You left, all was lost) from *Maachis* (1996) captures the same intensity using the simplest of words. There is also repentance as in the song '*Hazar rahein mud ke dekhi*' (Searched a thousand paths) from *Thodi si Bewafai* (1980).

There are songs where nature is touched upon with a kind of reverence: '*Hawaon pe likh do hawaon ke naam*' (Inscribe on the breeze, the name of the breeze) from *Biwi aur Makaan* (1966) or '*Woh shaam kuch ajeeb thi*' (That evening was strange) from *Khamoshi* (1969). In both these songs, the poet beckons different aspects of nature to be in tune with love and the lover. Similarly, the song '*Gulmohar 'gar naam hota*' (Had your name been Gulmohar) from *Devta* (1978) connects the gulmohar tree and its beauty with that of the lover. *Omkara's* (2006) '*O saathi re*' is an example of lovers asking nature to conspire with their love and help them conceal it from others.

Political satires

In the world of songs in Hindustani cinema, where it is romance that rules, Gulzar penned a couple of memorable songs which are a commentary on the political situation of the country. '*Haal chaal theek thaak hai*' (I am doing fine) from his directorial debut, *Mere Apne* (1971) is an ironic commentary about the conditions of the unemployed youth. Meanwhile, the song '*Salaam kijiye*' (Pay your respects) from *Aandhi* (1975) is a satire when a politician who hasn't brought about any significant change in the last five years of her rule, is taunted for she is back, asking for votes. Gulzar's last film as director, *Hu Tu Tu* (1999) has the most number of political songs – all of them throwing light on different aspects of the political situation of the country. If '*Jaago jaago jaagte raho*' (Wake up, keep awake) urges the common man to notice the wrongdoings of the politicians and the administration, '*Ghapla hai*' (Something is fishy) emphasizes on loopholes in the system, and '*Bandobast hai*' (We are prepared) is about how the common man has rolled up his sleeves to rise and fight against various social evils. Being a sensitive person, Gulzar has not remained untouched by India's changing political climate. It doesn't come across as a coincidence that all three films referred to here, have had him at the helm as director.

Songs for children

Gulzar admits that he has a special connection with children and one cannot deny that when he writes for them, the listener is transported to a world of innocence. Although the song '*Ek tha bachpan*' (Once there was childhood) from *Aashirwad* (1969) is not for children per se, it peeks into childhood as no other song does, with reminiscences from a blissful past. Regarding songs for children, '*Saare ke saare*' (All of us) from *Parichay* (1972) is a great example. It is playful and instructive, wrapped in a fun package introducing the basic musical notes and picturized with children at a picnic.

Then there are songs which showcase the effervescence of children and growing up. For example, '*Master ji ki aa gai chitthi*' (The teacher has received a letter) from *Kitaab* (1978), '*Lakdi ki kaathi, kaathi pe ghoda*' (A wooden horse) from *Masoom* (1982) and '*Chupdi chupdi chachi*' (A sticky chachi) from *Chachi 420* (1997). *Makdee* (2003) has two songs for children: '*Chhutti hai*' is about the excitement children feel the moment they get a day off from school and '*Panga na le*' (Don't mess with us) warns elders to not underestimate children or mess with them.

Gulzar has also penned a prayer – '*Hum ko mann ki shakti dena*' (Dear God, make our hearts strong) for the film *Guddi* (1971) which became so popular that even today it is taught and sung in morning assemblies in schools all over India. Similarly, the lullaby he wrote for *Sadma* (1983), '*Surmaiyee akhiyon mein nanha munna ek sapna de jaa re*' (Put a tiny dream in these kohl-rimmed eyes), continues to be a favourite amongst mothers to put infants to bed. Gulzar has penned poems and stories for television, the most popular one being the opening song for the animated television series, *Jungle Book*. The lines go as, *Jungle jungle baat chali hai, pata chala hai/Chaddi pahen ke phool khila hai, phool khila hai* (There is a rumour, everyone in the jungle knows/ A fresh flower has bloomed in innocent nakedness). Many raised their eyebrows on the use of language – specifically, bringing in the word '*chaddi*'(underwear) in a children's poem. The anecdote goes that the Board of the Children's Film Society – the production house for this series – was against it and tried to persuade Gulzar to replace this particular word. Gulzar, as usual, had the same defence that he has had for the choice of words in his other film poetry – the circumstance. He defended the word and refused to give an alternative, saying that an abandoned child in the jungle could either be picturized in an underwear or in nothing! It was the then Chairperson of the Children's Film Society, Jaya Bachchan who came to his rescue and helped let the song go as was originally composed. Of course, the song went on to become one of the most popular title songs to be used in any television series.[5]

These examples prove that Gulzar's poetry for children wasn't confined to the domain of cinema alone; it travelled and found its way in the lives of the masses. It is this connection that he has managed to establish, and that remains the source of his popularity.

Based on folklore, legends and classical poetry

On several occasions, Gulzar has taken the liberty to develop songs from couplets by his favourite Urdu poets – Ghalib,

---

5   In conversation, Gulzar with Vishal Bharadwaj, at the 11th Osian's Film Festival 2009.

Mir and Amir Khusrau – aiming to connect the classical with the contemporary. The first example that comes to mind is '*Dil dhoondta hai phir wohi fursat ke raat din*' (The heart seeks those days of leisure, once again) from *Mausam* (1976) where the opening couplet is Ghalib's. '*Sunai deti hai dil ki dhadkan*' (I can hear the heart beating) from *Ghulami* (1987) opens with a Persian couplet by Khusrau. Similarly, the song '*Satrangi re*' (O the rainbow-hued one) from *Dil Se* (1998) has Ghalib's couplet, '*Ishq par zor nahin*' (There is no control over love), woven within the song. Another example is from *Kaminey* (2009) where he has used Jigar Moradabadi's, '*Yeh ishq nahin aasaan*' (Love isn't easy) and moulded it as per the song's requirement.

Gulzar referred to Waris Shah's Heer Ranjha in the song, '*Ranjha Ranjha na kar Heeriye*' (O Heer, don't lament over Ranjha) from *Raavan* (2010). Again, he mentioned Heer along with Mirza Sahiba, another Punjabi folktale, in the song, '*Heer*' from *Jab Tak Hai Jaan* (2011).

Philosophical songs

Intrigued about the vagaries of life, Gulzar has tried to make sense of its mysteries in his own inimitable way. One such example is the song '*Tujhse naraaz nahin zindagi, hairan hoon main*' (O life, you do not upset me, but intrigue me) from *Masoom* (1982). '*Aane wala pal jaane wala hai*' (The moment which is about to come, will soon be gone) from *Gol Maal* (1979) and '*Yeh lamha filhaal jee lene de*' (Let me live this moment) from *Filhaal* (2002) reflect his philosophy of living in the present and making the most of it. The acceptance of life, with all its shortcomings, is what shines through in '*Thoda hai, thode ki zaroorat hai*' (I have some, I need some) from *Khatta Meetha* (1977). But the song which beseeches life to embrace oneself is '*Aye zindagi gale laga le*' (O life, embrace me) from *Sadma* (1983).

Gulzar has penned around five hundred songs and classifying and categorizing all of them is beyond the scope of this book. However, this was a small effort to bring a few of them together to understand his oeuvre. The best song to end this section on Gulzar's journey as a film poet should be '*Jai ho*' (Praise to be), from *Slumdog Millionaire* (2009) not because of the Grammy and the Oscar glory it earned, but because it is a song that truly celebrates life.

Gulzar's journey as a filmmaker

Gulzar has directed seventeen films. His involvement in them has not just always been as that of a director. He has written the stories (many a time, he has even adapted them from classical Indian literature), the dialogues, screenplays and of course, the songs. *Aandhi* was made in 1975 and by then, he was already about eighty songs old, the prominent ones being from films like *Biwi aur Makan* (1966), *Do Dooni Char* (1968), *Rahgir* (1969), *Khamoshi* (1969), *Aashirwad* (1969), *Guddi* (1971), *Seema* (1971), *Anubhav* (1971) and *Anand* (1973).

As a director, *Aandhi* was Gulzar's fifth film. He made his directorial debut with the critically acclaimed *Mere Apne* (1971). A remake of Tapan Sinha's *Apanjon*, this was the story of a widow, Aanandi Devi (played by Meena Kumari – this was to be her last film) who moves to the city to live with her nephew. Later, she moves out when she realizes why her nephew and his wife had made her stay with them – to take care of their house and their little son. After she leaves, Nani maa, as she is fondly called by some street children, starts living with them and finds herself involved in a gang war of two unemployed young men – Shyam (played by Vinod Khanna) and Chhennu (played by Shatrughan Sinha). The film ends with the death of Nani maa as she is caught between the cross-firing of the two gangs.

Mere Apne was unique in several ways. The protagonist was in her eighties. There was hardly any romantic angle woven in the story. The emphasis was on the youth unrest in the early 1970s. Although the original film was set in Bengal, Gulzar's adaptation took it to Allahabad.

The next venture was *Achanak* (1972), based on a story by Khwaja Ahmad Abbas, 'The Thirteenth Victim' (often mistakenly referred to as a film based on the famous Nanavati trial). A songless film, it talks of the strong intention of the filmmaker, as the producers and distributors, especially at that time, banked on the songs and their popularity for a film's success. The film was about the emotional turbulence of a man who is deeply in love with his wife, only to discover that she is having an extramarital affair in his absence, which finally leads him to kill her. The highlight of the film's screenplay is the change in the emotional graph of the protagonist.

Gulzar went on to make more 'off-beat' films like *Parichay* (1972) and *Koshish* (1972) before he made *Aandhi*. While *Parichay* (1972) was adapted from the Hollywood film, *Sound of Music* (1965), *Koshish* (1972) was based on the love, life and struggles of a couple who are mute and hearing impaired, brilliantly played by Sanjeev Kumar and Jaya Bachchan.

Both films were distinct in their own way, winning awards and the hearts of the masses. *Parichay* was the first film where Gulzar and music director R.D. Burman worked together, and thus began a memorable collaboration of fascinating melodies and profound lyrics. *Koshish's* screenplay fetched Gulzar his first National Award. Despite back-to-back commercial successes, it is important to emphasize that Gulzar didn't make these films using any templated commercial film formula. Neither were they completely off-beat films. It appeared as if he had even managed to confuse – and please – critics and audiences by making films that were in a unique and new genre of their own.

Gulzar's next film was *Aandhi* in 1975, a year which happens to be an important one in the history of Hindustani cinema. It is quite apt to call it the watershed year of Hindustani cinema – prolific in terms of commercial successes and diverse in the kind of range it offered. It was as much a year of blockbusters like *Sholay* and *Deewar* as it was of superhits like *Julie*, *Mili*, *Nishant*, *Amanush*, *Chupke Chupke* and *Jai Santoshi Maa*. Amitabh Bachchan and Sanjeev Kumar were both vying for the award for the Best Actor and inspite of the success of *Deewar*, the Filmfare Award went to Sanjeev Kumar for his role in *Aandhi*. (Three years later, the two actors were once more in contest for the same award, except this time it was Amitabh Bachchan who received the honour for *Amar Akbar Anthony* [1978].)

Having said that, the year 1975 was Gulzar's year – he had three releases, one after the other, all of them strikingly different and in a class of their own; all with the characteristic Gulzar stamp.

After *Aandhi*, Gulzar's next film was *Mausam* (1975), in which he explored yet another dimension of the man–woman relationship. There's a story behind the timing of both these films. Gulzar said, 'On *Aandhi*'s premiere, I was shooting for *Mausam*, and on *Mausam*'s premiere I was shooting for *Aandhi*.'[6] It so happened that Gulzar finished shooting *Aandhi* and by the time it was about to release in theatres, he had started shooting for *Mausam*. However, when the controversy around *Aandhi* erupted (discussed at length in the next chapter), he had to make a couple of additions and deletions to the film. So, it was during this

---

6   From the interview appended in the book.

second session of shooting for *Aandhi* that *Mausam* had its premiere. *Mausam* was adapted from the novel, *The Judas Tree* by A.J. Cronin, a Scottish novelist. It fetched Gulzar the National Award for the Second Best Feature Film and the Filmfare Award for Direction while *Aandhi* got him the Filmfare Critics' Award for Best Film.

Khushboo (1975), Gulzar's third film that year was culled out from Saratchandra Chatterjee's Bengali story 'Pandit Moshay'. Instead of adapting the entire story, Gulzar extracted from it a linear storyline and wove the entire film around it. It is a story of a spirited woman, and the film can be labelled as one of the precursors of feminist cinema.

Kitaab (1978), which also happens to be one of Gulzar's favourites, was also adapted from Bengali literature and this time, it was Samaresh Basu's 'Pothik' (Traveller), a story about a young boy who stays with his sister and brother-in-law. It is narrated as seen from the eyes of the boy. Another story by Basu that Gulzar adapted for screen was 'Akal Bashonto' (Untimely Spring) which he named *Namkeen* (1981). What is characteristic of these films, like all of Gulzar's work, is that they were not only strikingly different from the films his contemporaries were making at the time, but even individually, they were different from each other.

Kinara (1977) was based on Bhushan Banmali's story, which in turn was inspired by a Hollywood film, *Magnificent Obsession*. The legend of Baaz Bahadur and Rani Roopmati has been woven beautifully in it, along with the love story of Inder and Arti. This film also received acclaim – both critically, as well as commercially.

Inspired by William Shakespeare's *A Comedy of Errors*, Gulzar made *Angoor* (1980), a film now considered a timeless comedy. Although a film titled *Do Dooni Chaar* with a storyline similar to that of *Angoor* had already been made earlier in 1968 by Debu Sen, where Gulzar was involved as a writer, it was not commercially successful. Therefore Gulzar wanted to make it again. This time, his treatment helped the film successfully connect with the masses.

Gulzar delved into history too and the outcome was *Meera* (1979), the story of a sixteenth-century Rajasthani princess who was in love with Lord Krishna, and devoted her life singing hymns in his praise. Once again, it is the woman protagonist, whom Gulzar made all powerful and gave the strength to revolt against the existing norms of a royal family.

Gulzar's *Ijaazat* (1986) is based on a Bengali short story by Subodh Ghosh, where for the first time in Hindustani cinema, an extramarital affair has been dealt with in a mature manner; the wife and the 'other woman', both seemed to be right in their own places and were equally loved by the audiences. The male hero too had the audience's sympathy. The song '*Mera kuch samaan*' (Some of my belongings) continues to be a favourite amongst listeners. It went on to win both the National Award and the Filmfare Award.

Lekin (1991) is based on a short story by Tagore, 'Kshudito Pashaan', and is about a government official (played by Vinod Khanna) posted in a village in Rajasthan, where he meets a woman, Reva (played by Dimple Kapadia). Her character, though, is shrouded in mystery and one keeps guessing if Reva is real or just a figment of his imagination. The film is a saga of time and birth, and took the audiences to Rajasthan, beautifully captured among the sand dunes and old havelis.

If *Maachis* is a sequel of sorts to *Mere Apne*, *Hu Tu Tu* seems to be a follow-up to *Aandhi*. It is not just the passing of time, but through his films, Gulzar has tried to bring to the forefront the changes that came about in the sociopolitical fabric of the country. The small-town politics, led by the unemployed youth who are dissatisfied with society at large in *Mere Apne* eventually go on to show how the same youth are exploited and revolt against the political establishment. Their level of anger seems to increase over time, keeping with the changing political scenario in the country. *Maachis* is also a telling statement of the political situation prevailing in Punjab at the time. It brought together the combination on Gulzar and Vishal Bhardwaj for the first time in films, which went on to give many memorable scores. *Hu Tu Tu* seems to take off twenty-five years following *Aandhi*. If there was a woman politician in the latter, who gave up her family life to continue her career in politics, *Hu Tu Tu* is from the perspective of the daughter of a politician who uses unscrupulous ways to reach the heights where she finally reached.

Having briefly touched upon the repository of Gulzar 's work, let us come back to the film in focus, *Aandhi*.

Synopsis

Set against a political backdrop of the elections and politicking between various parties and politicians, *Aandhi* is a love story between a hotel manager and his ambitious wife who aspires to be a minister one day. If this man–woman relationship has love, humour and sacrifice on the one hand, there is ego and ambition on the other. The couple has differences due to their very contrasting personalities. Using the oft-used technique of the flashback, a favoured tool with Gulzar, the screenplay moves through different planes, comparing the two protagonists and revealing the contrasts in the way various issues are experienced by a married couple. Both the headstrong, individualistic protagonists develop into mature characters as the story enfolds.

The opening scene, when the credits are rolling, sets the tone of the film. Different parties are shown canvassing for their respective candidates. Finally, the attention is on the protagonist of the film, Aarti Devi, who plans to visit her constituency. As luck would have it, she comes to stay in the same hotel where JK, her estranged husband, is the manager, obviously oblivious to this fact. However, she is surprised to find things of her taste in the room she checks into (a surahi instead of a flask, chandan agarbattis and so on) puzzling her beyond words, till she comes face to face with him. She visits him in the evening and together they remember the days when they were together, and how they drifted apart. Soon, Aarti Devi's visit to JK in the evening becomes a daily ritual during her stay at the hotel. They even go out. This portion of the film concentrates on the ebb and tide of their relationship, their first meeting, the entanglement and finally the reasons why they parted ways. Moving parallelly is the narrative of the changing dynamics of the political climate across the country. The role of the print media is particularly highlighted. Aarti Devi is attacked by a mob and gets hit on the forehead. The press conference that follows this attack, is a very interesting satire on the political situation of the country, the role of the opposition and the place of the *aam janta*, the masses. The opposition party gets a whiff of Aarti Devi's meetings with JK and attempts to play up a scandal to tarnish her reputation. The film ends with Aarti giving a fiery speech about the sacrifices she had made in her personal life to be in politics, 'to serve humanity'. She acknowledges the presence of her husband, who in turn sees her off as she proceeds to complete her election campaign.

The film was based on a story written by Kamleshwar, a popular Hindi author[7] (with twelve novels including *Kitne Pakistan* [2000] and seventeen collections of short stories to his credit) and scriptwriter, who had composed other well-known films such as *Mausam, Chhoti Si Baat* and *Amanush* that released in the same year as *Aandhi* (1975). He also wrote the story of *Rang Birangi* (1983) and dialogues for *The Burning Train* (1980), *Souten* (1983), *Yeh Desh* (1984) and *Preeti* (1986), amongst others. He even penned serials like *Chandrakanta* and *Yug* for the state broadcaster, Doordarshan.

Forty years after its release, *Aandhi* is still remembered for the talent of Suchitra Sen, Sanjeev Kumar, R.D. Burman and, of course, Gulzar. Although it generated a controversy over the protagonist's resemblance to the then prime minister, Indira Gandhi, and was even banned for a while, it is not a political film. Dealing with the relationship between a man and his wife, *Aandhi* is one of the finest films to explore the tussle between patriarchal and individualistic values, unravelling effortlessly the layers in a complex relationship.

---

7   Harihar Swarup, 'Kamleshwar Brings Out the Truth of Life', http://www.tribuneindia.com/2003/20031228/edit.htm#3, accessed on 10 October 2013.

chapter two

The Controversy

The period between 26 June 1975 and 21 March 1977 is considered one of the most turbulent phases in free India and it affected the entire nation. The then prime minister, Indira Gandhi, requested the then president Fakhruddin Ali Ahmed to declare Emergency, resulting in the suspension of elections as well as all other civil liberties and rights. In an article in the *Indian Express*[8], a handwritten note dated 8 January 1975 by the then chief minister of West Bengal, S.S. Ray to Indira Gandhi is quoted which alludes to the possibility that the decision to impose Emergency was pre-decided.

---

8 Manoj CG, 'SS Ray to Indira Gandhi six months before Emergency: Crack down, get law ready', *The Indian Express*, 13 June 2015, http://indianexpress.com/article/india/india-others/six-months-before-emergency-s-s-ray-to-indira-gandhi-crack-down-get-law-ready/, accessed on 7 January 2016.

If one looks at the political cauldron from the beginning of that year, one can see things bubbling and simmering. In an exhaustive study of the period, the British sociologist David Lockwood (2016) brought forth the condition of the country during that time, the opposition which slowly gained majority over the ruling party and the actual course of the Emergency. It was on 12 June 1975 that Justice Jagmohanlal Sinha of the Allahabad High Court convicted Indira Gandhi of corrupt campaign practices, resulting from a case brought by Raj Narain, her opponent in the 1971 elections.[9] On 25 June 1975, at a massive opposition rally in Delhi, Jayaprakash Narayan, one of the fiercest opponents of the ruling party, announced that the Janata Party would not allow Gandhi to function as prime minister, and a massive civil disobedience movement would commence from 29 June.[10] However, before such a movement could begin, the government declared the Emergency under Article 352 of the Indian Constitution.

It was in this political backdrop that *Aandhi* was released. While the other films of the year were released either before or after the Emergency was imposed, *Aandhi*, although officially released prior to the Emergency, was banned in its twenty-third week during the Emergency. However, it

---

9   D. Lockwood, *The Communist Party and the Indian* Emergency, New Delhi: Sage Publications, 2016, p. 111.

10 Ibid., p. 112.

was back in theatres with minor cuts and additions again during the Emergency itself. Gulzar himself was surprised about the ban. At that time he was in Moscow, attending a film festival where *Aandhi* was also being screened, and he learnt that he would have to pull out of the show as the film had been banned in India. To be sure, it was a film magazine that had published a feature on *Aandhi*, with the headline, 'See your Prime Minister on screen'. Gulzar had to rush back to India and remove a few scenes and shoot some new ones. In one of the additional scenes, Aarti Devi, the protagonist, looks at a framed portrait of Indira Gandhi claiming that she was her ideal. William Mazzarella, in his book *Censorium: Cinema and the Open Edge of Mass Publicity*, discusses various issues of censorship in cinema. The key questions he probes are:

> What is the place of affective intensities in modern mass-mediated democracies? What is the importance of the fact that we are called upon to belong at once to concrete crowds and to abstract publics? And what happens to political authority when it can no longer reside in the physical body of a singular sovereign and has to find its feet in the intimately anonymous space of mass publicity? (p. 4)[11]

---

11 Quoted in Erin O'Donnell, 'Making Sense of Censorship: Censorium: Cinema and the Open Edge of Mass Publicity, by William Mazzarella', *Senses of Cinema*, June 2014, http://

Gulzar himself asserts that he did not make the film and base Aarti Devi's character on Indira Gandhi.[12] Yes, the character drew on her personality, only with regard to the aspect of how she would descend the stairs, get off the helicopter or walk briskly, but nothing beyond that. Shoma A. Chatterji, in her book *Suchitra Sen: The Legend and the Enigma*, quotes the actor herself, who insists that she did not fashion the character after Indira Gandhi.[13]

The 1970s were a turbulent and volatile era with the cinema of the period being associated with the image of the 'angry young man'[14]. In fact, writer Nikhat Kazmi in *Ire in the Soul: Bollywood's Angry Years* calls the decade 'Bollywood's angry years'. The growing desolation and disillusionment of the public had begun to manifest itself in cinema in myriad ways. While the decade saw the rise

---

sensesofcinema.com/2014/book-reviews/making-sense-of-censorship-censorium-cinema-and-the-open-edge-of-mass-publicity-by-william-mazzarella/, accessed on 7 January 2016.

12 See 'Where is reality?', *The Hindu*, 20 July 2001, https://www.thehindu.com/thehindu/2001/07/20/stories/09200221.htm, accessed on 17 December 2018.

13 S. Chatterji, *Suchitra Sen: The Legend and the Enigma*, New Delhi: HarperCollins Publishers, 2015, p. 33.

14 The term 'angry young man' was initially coined for Jimmy Porter, the protagonist of John Osborne's play, *Look Back in Anger* (1956). However, this term has also been used for Amitabh Bachchan and his films of 1970s.

of Amitabh Bachchan as *the* angry young man, it also witnessed films that were mellower but had a seething rage within. *Aandhi* was one of those films. Anger was replacing the socialism of the 1950s and the romance of 1960s. After one war with China (1962) and two with Pakistan (1965 and 1971), the economic resources of the nation were rather drained, resulting in the rise of discontent and anger against the prevailing political establishment at the time.

Starting with the textual analysis of the film, one can say that the opening scene of *Aandhi* sets the tone of the film. The title credits feature a montage of scenes from a typical election campaign – speeches, banners, canvassing, visits by politicians, slogan shouting through the loudspeakers tied to jeeps, and so on and so forth. The first dialogue is by a politician. He claims:

> '*Yakeen maniye, mujhe shauk nahin hai election ladne ka. Aur na hee mujhe kisi doctor ne kaha hai election ladne ko. Lekin mujhe election ladna padta hai apne huqooq ke liye, Janata ke huqooq ke liye…*'
>
> (Believe me, it isn't my hobby to fight elections. Nor has any doctor advised me to do so. But I have to fight elections for my rights, for the rights of the common man…)

How this politician claims that he wishes to contest the elections only for the sake of humanity and not for his personal gain is something that the story further reveals. He plays it dirty, maligning Aarti Devi, his opponent, to win the elections and the entire exercise seems to indicate how in politics, people can reach their goal by all means possible.

In *Deewaar: The Footpath, the City and the Angry Young Man*, Vinay Lal talks about the political scenario of the country in 1975. Of the many films that became a blockbuster that year, *Deewaar* was the one of the first, releasing in January. Lal points out, 'Unrest was widespread: economic productivity had declined precipitously, cities were crippled by strikes and protests, and political unrest would underscore the fragile nature of the Indian state.'[15] It is this state of the nation that Gulzar too portrays in *Aandhi* (released in February that year), where the 'fragile' political situation of the country forms the backdrop for the central plot, a love story.

In many ways, *Aandhi* captures the essence of the political, social as well as economic changes of that decade. It reflects the unrest in a civil society marked by elections, the ill-intentions of various political parties, youth unrest and their dissatisfaction. But the film has a strange equation with reality. Nowhere, through the course of the film, does one see the political theme overriding the love story, or vice-versa. The balance between the two is profound,

15 V. Lal, *Deewaar: The Footpath, the City and the Angry Young Man*, New Delhi: HarperCollins Publishers, 2011, p. 3.

and the filmmaker successfully communicates both the elements with ease.

Anirudh Deshpande, in 'Indian Cinema and Bourgeois State'[16] claims that Indian cinema is neither politically innocent nor conveys an unequivocal secularism. He tries to trace how cinema in colonial India was affected by censorship and elite preferences. As the end of British colonialism brought the Indian bourgeoisie to power and seriously started the process of nation building, it began to reflect in Indian cinema as well. In Deshpande's opinion, the more apolitical a film pretended to be, the greater was its political significance. *Aandhi* was one film where even the undertones of romance were loaded with shades of politics.

An apt example of that is a regular conversation between a man and his wife, in this case Aarti Devi and JK, and one can see their distinct views on patriotism and the idea of revolution. In the scene where JK gets burned by a steaming cup of tea, and Aarti is applying ointment on his feet, she sarcastically remarks:

'*Khud hee kahte the, inqalaabi aag par bhi chal sakte hain, ab kya hua?*'

(You yourself used to say, revolutionaries can walk on burning charcoals. What happened now?)

---

16 *Economic and Political Weekly*, Vol. 42, No. 5 (Dec 15–21, 2007), pp. 99–101; 103.

JK – '*Bina karan koi aag mein nahin koodta. Barah saal ka tha jab apni party ke liye goli khayee thi.*'

(No one jumps into fire without a reason. I was only twelve when I had faced a bullet for my party.)

Aarti – '*Ab kyun* party *ke khilaaf ho?*'

(Then why are you against the party now?)

JK – '*Us waqt inqalaabi* party *thi. Inqalaab ke liye ladte the…*'

(It used to be a revolutionary party then. We were fighting for a revolution…)

Aarti – '*Ab bhi to usi ke liye* fight *karte hain.*'

(We still fight for that.)

JK – '*Huh … hartal, satyagrah, bhala iss tarah inqalaab aata hai?*'

(Huh … strike, political resistance … does a revolution happen like this?)

Aarti – '*Ab tak to usi se aayein hain…*'

(That is how revolutions have happened till now.)

JK – '*Ab tum bahas na karna shuru kar do … kyunki tumne* BA, MA *politics mein kiya hai … chodo pair mere*'

(Now don't you start arguing ... just because you have done some BA, MA in politics ... now leave my feet.)

Aarti (smiling) – '*Badi der laga di aapne pair chhudane mein*'
(You took so long in taking your feet away.)

JK – '*Yeh dekha ... yehi* politics *hai ... issi ko* politics *kahte hain ... issi liye mujhe isse nafrat hain ... jahan imaandari na chale, wahan mere liye kuch nahin chalta*'
(See this ... this is politics ... this is what politics is ... that is why I hate it so much ... I can't stay where there is no honesty)

Through a simple conversation between a husband and wife about the nature of politics and how their points of view differ, Gulzar very poignantly brings out the essence of politics. One might argue that broadly, politics is all about waiting for the opportune moment and taking advantage of the situation. If at one level, JK and Aarti were discussing why JK was now against politics although he himself was a part of it while growing up, on the other level, the 'politics of a relationship' also shines through in their conversation.

In another scene in the film, when Aarti tells her father about her intention of getting married, his response is that of shock and disgust:

K. Bose – *'Padh likh kar agar gul khilane the to Oxford mein jaa kar paanch saal zaaya karne ki kya zaroorat thi?'*

(What was the need of wasting five years in Oxford, if you had to end up doing this?)

(Pointing at the photograph of Indira Gandhi) Do you know, what sacrifices were given by this girl? If big ambitions are to be achieved, you have to forgo these trivial pleasures.

Aarti – *'Yehi to meri* ideal *hain…'*

(She is the one, who is my ideal.)

K. Bose – *'Main chahta hoon tum* politics *mein jao. Kuch* position *haasil karo … taake mere* business *ko bhi kuch fayda pahunche … tum samjhti nahin ho … tumhari taraqqi hogee, to mere* business *ki bhi taraqqi hogee. Aaj kal to* politics *ke bina to kuch…'*

(I want you to join politics … have a position of your own … so that even my business profits from it … you don't understand … my business will improve if you grow … there is nothing without politics these days…)

Aarti – *'Main rajneeti mein ja rahi thi to desh ki sewa ke liye, aapki dukaan chalane ke liye nahin, aur chod rahi hoon, to apna ghar basane ke liye.'*

(When I was entering politics, it was to serve the country, not to run your business. And if today, I am quitting it, it is to set up my home.)

It becomes clear that Aarti is very sure about where she stands with regard to politics and business. She does not wish to be scrupulous; her sole intention is to serve the country and its people.

However, all politicians in the film do not follow her ideology. Her opponent, Chandra Sen, employs every trick in the book to bring Aarti Devi down. When he gets a whiff of her meeting with the 'hotel manager', her frequent visits to his house or even going out with him, he tells a photographer to trail her and capture evidence. Sen goes to the extent of getting the photos made into posters and has them pasted all over the city.

Chandra Sen is not the only one who is portrayed as someone who adopts unsavoury methods to get his way. Within Aarti's political party itself, there is Lallu Laal, who is depicted as someone who often plays games to pull in some votes. He also makes sure that Aarti Devi doesn't get to know of his doings. One such activity is when he provokes Agarwal, an industrialist, to stand for the elections, so that their party can garner votes not only from the mill workers, but also from the mill owners. To be sure, Lallu Laal's intention is only to break up Chandra Sen's votebank. If the votes of both the working class and the mill owners go to Agarwal, it would brighten Aarti Devi's chances of winning the elections. Interestingly, when Chandra Sen gets to know of Lallu Laal's manipulative ways, he becomes furious but calms down as soon as he learns of a workers' strike in one of Agarwal's mills; in fact, he then tells his party's workers to make sure that the strike continues.

Such is the situation of the country depicted in *Aandhi* – the so-called leaders are only concerned about how to win elections. It is Aarti Devi who is surprised when Agarwal contests the elections and wonders if this was all Lallu Laal's plan. She advises him:

> *'Khayal rahe, Lallu Laal ji, jhoot se mujhe sakht nafrat hai. Jhoot bol kar sachchayee kabhi nahin jeeti ja sakti. Janta ko agar meri zaroorat hogee to mujhe apnaye gi. Aur nahin, to nikal ke phenk degi. Janta se koi chaal na chalna.'*

(Please remember, Lallu Laal ji, I hate lies. One cannot win over truth with lies. If the public wants me, it will embrace me. And if not, it will just throw me out. Never play games with the common man.)

The viewer gets an insight into Aarti's political ideology through her various actions and words peppered throughout the film. In another scene, there is a press conference where the exchange of words sums up the situation of the country. Several questions are asked by the members of the press, all related to the concerns brewing in the mind of the common man of that era. A journalist asks Aarti Devi, *'Is violence a part of politics?'* To which she replies, *'Certainly, violence is a part of bad politics.'* For the viewer, it is a line as simple as this that clears the air about the difference between good politics and bad politics. Aarti Devi not only accepts the fact that violence is associated with politics, but also concedes that it is a part of bad politics. Another question that she is asked is whether she feels that the leader of the opposition was behind the pelting of stones at her, to which she replies, '*Yeh kaam nafrat ka hai, chhotepan ka.*' (This is a deed of hatred, of lowliness.)

What Gulzar was trying to emphasize here was that although one sees bursts of violence all around, politics and violence do go hand in hand, although there is no need for it. Aarti Devi, in her reply to the last question, stresses on the fact that the common man has the power to oust anyone in power without resorting to violence.

JK, despite claiming to be someone who wants to stay away from the politics in the country at the time, too loses his temper when he hears Agarwal making derogatory remarks about Aarti Devi behind her back, some replete with sexual innuendo. Enraged, JK gets physical with him and threatens to throw him out of the hotel. While exiting the scene, he tells Aarti:

'I am not a bloody politician … *kisi mai ke laal mein himmat hai to aakar poochhe ki mera tumhara rishta kya hai … main jawab doonga … tumse kyun poochh rahe hain … aise oochhi harkatein tumhari siyasat mein chalti hongi … meri zindagi mein unke liye koi jagah nahin.*'

(I am not a bloody politician ... anyone who has the guts to find out, should come and ask me ... I will respond ... why are they asking you? ... Such cheap stunts may be acceptable in your world of politics ... I don't have place for such things in my life.)

JK storms out after this outburst.

There is obvious tension after this scene. However, everything falls in place when, at another election rally, Aarti addresses the public, disrupting Chander Sen's speech as he is mouthing accusations about her, and reveals the truth about her relationship with JK. Chander Sen, in his speech, brings to fore the aspects which in his opinion a good leader must possess:

'Jo log janta ke leader banna chahte hain, unhe janta ke saamne uncha aadarsh rakhna padta hai. Kuch aise kaam bhi karne padte hain ki janta unki izzat kare, unka aadar kare. Aur jo log aisa nahin kar sakte, unhe janta ke saamne se nikal jaana chahiye.'

(All those who wish to be leaders, need to possess certain qualities. They also need to do certain things so that the public can respect them, admire them. And, those who can't do this, they should not claim to be leaders, and move away from the lives of the public.)

To this, Aarti responds by appealing to the masses gathered there:

> '*Nyay kijiye, aur doshi samjhiye to kadi se kadi saza dijiye mujhe ... main inse das baras baad mili kyunki pichle das baras se main aapke saath hoon. Aapki takleef, aapke sukh dukh baatne ke liye ... aapke beech rehne ki, aapke saath rahne ki bahut badi qeemat chukayi hai maine....*'

(Please do justice. And punish me, if you find me guilty ... I met him after ten years because I have been with you for the last ten years, to share your pain and sorrows ... I have paid a heavy price for staying amidst you, for being by your side...)

Aarti Devi pleads to the public and asks them to punish her if they think she was at fault, thus winning over the sympathy of the masses. And it is this sympathy that leads to votes and helps her win the elections.

☙

It is important to emphasize here that it is baseless to get into a debate about whether *Aandhi* has been modelled on the life of Indira Gandhi. Sure, there are similarities. Apart from the fact that the character and features of Aarti Devi are largely borrowed from Mrs Gandhi's style (including the brisk walk and her large dialed-watch), it is striking that both Aarti Devi and Mrs Gandhi had an estranged marriage.

If stones were pelted at Aarti Devi at a rally, they were also pelted at Mrs Gandhi in 1967 at a rally near Bhubaneswar, Orissa. It is this coincidence about the estranged marriage, and the fact that Feroze Gandhi too ran a hotel in Allahabad that led the critics and viewers to connect the dots and begin to believe that *Aandhi* was the story of Indira Gandhi.

A viewer can see the film at two levels, both mingling with and intersecting each other. One is about the rekindling of lost love between Aarti and JK, and the other as a statement on the political climate of the country. At all points of conflict between the couple (during their early married life or even after their estrangement), the reason has always been the same – the notion of politics and how differently they see it. In his article, 'Pictures, Emotions, Conceptual Change', Imke Rajamani points out to a similar fact that no other form of media in the 1970s and 1980s is comparable in its outreach and impact on the male urban population of the lower and middle classes as popular cinema.[17] Keeping this theoretical framework in mind, one can easily infer that *Aandhi* represented the political turmoil that was brewing in the country in the first half of the decade. If there was one political leader who was thinking about the betterment of the society, without

17 Imke Rajamani, 'Pictures, Emotions, Conceptual Change: Anger in Popular Cinema', *Contribution to the History of Concepts*, Vol. 7, No. 2, 2012, pp. 52–77.

indulging in unscrupulous actions, her opponents as well as her own party workers were not thinking on the same lines. The conflict of ideologies is apparent in every frame of the film. The frustration of the common man is evident. They question their leaders and want to know how their leaders are treating them (an apt representation of this is the satirical qawwali in the film, discussed at length in chapter 4). However, they can be easily manipulated and instigated. At one point, when handed eggs to throw at a rally, it is worth noting that each egg is wrapped in a ten-rupee note. Lallu Laal asks the people to keep the tenner and throw the egg at the politician and disrupt his speech. Gullible as they are, people do as told.

Partha Chatterjee opens the essay 'Indian Cinema: Then and Now' with the line, 'Cinema, it is said, is usually a fair indicator of a nation's psyche, which may possibly be responsible for its (current) state of being, and which in turn, may be affected by the turn of historical, political and economic events in a given frame of time.'[18] *Aandhi*, yet again, follows this as a thumb rule and depicts the political nerve of the country.

The film ends with Aarti Devi walking into a rally by her opponent and and it is here that she wins over the people with her emotional speech about her sacrificing her

---

18 Partha Chatterjee, 'Indian Cinema: Then and Now', *India International Centre Quarterly*, Vol. 39, No. 2, 2012, p. 45.

personal life to serve the country. The people attending the rally are seen wiping tears and it is obvious that there is no looking back for her, as far as winning the elections were concerned. The following scene shows Aarti and JK listening to the news of the election results. She wins by a huge margin.

Aandhi ends with JK seeing off Aarti as she goes back to her professional world. The film completes a full circle – it begins with a scene depicting an election campaign and ends with an election victory.

chapter three

The Stellar Cast

ॐ

Cinema is an art form which depicts reality in its own way. It has its own distinguishing characteristics and mechanics to do so. If other arts like painting or writing are forms of expression of a single person, a film involves a team, and that makes the sense of expression complicated and difficult. The vision of the filmmaker can only come through when he can successfully pass it on first to his/her crew members, who then bring that vision to life using their expertise. There are certain art forms which involve mechanical tools, but need artistic intervention, talent and craftsmanship for an idea to blossom. Photography is one example. And then, there are certain processes which entirely depend on the skill of the individual – an actor's performance is one such area. The link between the filmmaker and the actor is crucial. It is the filmmaker's responsibility to communicate his vision to the actors, and it is the actor's duty to realize that vision.

In *Aandhi*, performances by the cast members surpass all their other performances. Interestingly, although *Aandhi* is generally considered feminist cinema, there is only a single woman character in the film. That aspect aside, there aren't many characters in the film. Apart from the two protagonists, Aarti Devi and JK, there are some important roles – played by Rehman, A.K. Hangal, Om Prakash and Om Shivpuri – and all their characters are very well etched. In the book *Amar Akbar Anthony: Masala, Madness and Manmohan Desai*, Sidharth Bhatia talks about the importance of the supporting cast in any film. 'The supporting cast are crucial,' he writes. 'They enhance the film in many ways and [are] a good foil to the lead actors. A bad actor can destroy a scene; a good one strengthen it.'[19] This chapter looks at these cast members, first as actors and then as the characters they portrayed in *Aandhi*.

Suchitra Sen (1931–2014)

'Suchitra Sen was an era' is the opening sentence of Shoma A. Chatterji's book, *Suchitra Sen: The Legend and the Enigma*,

---

19 Siddharth Bhatia, *Amar Akbar Anthony: Masala, Madness and Manmohan Desai*, New Delhi: HarperCollins Publishers, 2013, p. 88.

quoting the journalist Ranjan Bandyopadhyay. A lot is established by this single line.

Suchitra Sen ruled Bengali cinema for decades and gave powerful performances in *Deep Jwele Jaai* (1959) and *Uttar Falguni* (1963) among many others. Beginning her career with *Shesh Kothay* (1952), she continued to give powerful peformances, one after the other, till the year 1978 when she quit cinema after *Pronoy Pasha* (1978). In Hindustani cinema, she is remembered for *Devdas* (1955), *Bombai ka Babu* (1960), *Mamta* (1966) and, of course, *Aandhi*. Although she acted in very few Hindi films, her ethereal beauty, screen presence and emotive powers led to her popularity among viewers, and she was considered at par with actresses who starred in many more films than her.

Sen's personal photographer, Dhiren Deb, claimed that he had never 'met a woman more decent, warmer, more beautiful, more complete and ideal' than her.[20] Chatterji writes that Suchitra's choice of roles indicated she was a woman with a mind of her own at a time when most actresses were happy doing whatever they were offered. Often, she played the role of a working woman, a rare phenomenon in those days.[21]

Maitreyee B. Chowdhury, in the book *Uttam Kumar and Suchitra Sen*, writes, 'Suchitra Sen evokes the image of a

---

20 Chatterji, *Suchitra Sen*, p. 25.
21 Ibid., p. 53.

woman of incredible beauty and grace, with large haunting eyes. Yet she remains an enigma.'[22] She adds, 'The way she dressed, her makeup, her way of talking, everything bespoke of a woman in command of herself and accustomed to attention.'[23]

Maybe this was the reason why Gulzar chose Suchitra Sen to play the role of Aarti Devi. The director himself says that he had always wanted to cast Suchitra Sen in a film, but decided to approach her only once he had written a role which suited her talent.[24] The persona of Aarti Devi's character was a good fit for Suchitra Sen's personality. Chatterji quotes an interesting anecdote between Gulzar and Suchitra Sen, highlighting the equation between the two – in that, both of them would address each other as 'Sir'. Although he was younger to Sen, in both 'age and experience', Gulzar says that she insisted in addressing him as 'Sir', much against the requests of Gulzar. So, he too started addressing her as 'Sir'. The two of them continued using this salutation with each other even after the film was wrapped up.[25] Chatterjee also quotes Gulzar and his

---

22 M.B. Chowdhury, *Uttam Kumar and Suchitra Sen: Bengali Cinema's First Couple*, New Delhi: OM Books International, 2013, p. 17.

23 Ibid., p. 20.

24 See interview appended in this book.

25 Chatterji, *Suchitra Sen*, p. 20.

remembering Sen as an 'extremely warm and a sensitive person'.[26]

Suchitra Sen as Aarti Devi

Suchitra Sen's entry as Aarti Devi sets the tone for how the audience perceives her character. Enigmatic and energetic, she climbs down the stairs with great aplomb. File in hand, a crisp cotton sari neatly tucked at her waist, dark glasses over her eyes and all this against a compelling background score make quite an impression in announcing the arrival of the film's protagonist.

To appreciate how she successfully switches her personality from an authoritative politician to a woman who meets her estranged love, credit must be go to Gulzar and Suchitra Sen. During the film, Sen portrays three different and very distinct traits of Aarti's personality. In one, she plays a young, free spirited woman who dares to fall in love, stands her ground in front of an opposing father, gets married, and eventually has a falling out with her husband. In the second, she plays a politician who has the strength to lead a country. All her moves are packed with positivity and energy. And in the third, she meets her estranged husband after a gap of nine years; the way she mellows down, the ache of heartbreak melts through her

---

26 Ibid., p. 25.

eyes. It is incredible for a character to go through so many transformations during a single film.

The portion of the film which is about the newly married life of the couple, depicts Aarti as a very carefree person. The relationship between the husband and wife is described using wit and humour, and at one point, JK acknowledges this when, laughing, he tells his colleague: 'You know, my wife has a classic sense of humour. *Main baap banne wala hoon … yehi baat mujhe subah ghar pe bata sakti thi*. Telegram *bheja hai usne…*' (You know, my wife has a classic sense of humour. I am going to be a father … she could have told me this in the morning, at home … but she has telegrammed this news to me.)

JK also comments on his wife's strength: 'You don't know the strength of my wife. *Woh mahinon ka kaam dinon mein karti hai* (She finishes the tasks that's generally done in months, in days). She will just do it like that' (he clicks his fingers). This again reflects the fact that JK knows very well the strength of his wife. He is fully aware of her strong temperament and her will to get things done, those which she wishes to accomplish.

Another feature of Aarti's character that comes through is that she has great respect for the common man and holds idealistic views of how to run the government. At one point, when she suspects Lallu Laal playing up some game, she tells him: '*Jhoot bol kar sachchayee kabhi nahin jeeti jaa sakti*' (Truth cannot be won with lies).

Towards the end of the film, when Aarti leaves the hotel in anger, JK remarks about her: 'She hasn't changed a single bit. *Wohi mizaaj, wohi ghussa, wohi* impulsive nature' (She hasn't changed a single bit. The same temperament, the same anger, the same impulsive nature).

To sum up on what the filmmaker himself had to say about his protagonist, Maitreyee B. Chowdhury quotes Gulzar and says that very few actresses could have lent the dignity that Suchitra did to the character of Aarti.[27]

Sanjeev Kumar (1938–1985)

Popularly known as 'Hari bhai' in the film fraternity, Sanjeev Kumar was an actor for all seasons, and worked with many filmmakers in his career. Being associated with IPTA (Indian People's Theatre Association), he started his career with theatre. He was barely 22 when he played the lead role in Arthur Miller's *All My Sons*. That role was of an old man, and as per a popular anecdote, even Prithviraj Kapoor did not recognize him and inquired about him. It was here that Gulzar spotted him too.

In his early years in the industry, Sanjeev Kumar did some character roles. His first film as a protagonist was *Nishan* (1965). However, it was *Khilona* (1970) which brought him recognition and acceptance in cinema. The frenzy and dedication with which he plays the part of a

---

27 Chowdhury, *Uttam Kumar and Suchitra Sen*, p. 54.

mentally challenged man is commendable. However, it was his association with Gulzar and the roles he essayed in his films that surpassed all the other ones. In public memory, he might be remembered most fondly for his character of Thakur Baldev Singh in *Sholay* (1975), and for roles in *Trishul* (1978), *Naya Din, Nayi Raat* (1974) and *Pati Patni aur Woh* (1978), but it is his characters in *Mausam* (1975), *Aandhi* (1975), *Angoor* (1982), *Namkeen* (1982) and *Koshish* (1972), and even a cameo in *Parichay* (1972) that outshine all his other roles. Gulzar said that Sanjeev Kumar understood the requirements of his role quite well.[28] Interestingly, if one observes the physical appearance of two characters played by Kumar in Gulzar's films, *Mausam* and *Aandhi*, both released in the same year, one will find them to be identical. Both characters are middle-aged and dress similarly. However, their personalities come across as drastically different. Such was his acting calibre. It was the equation between Sanjeev Kumar and Gulzar that led to the creation of the finer attributes of both personas on screen.

Sanjeev Kumar as JK

> '*Bilkul waise hee ho…*'
> (You are just the same.)

---

28 M.L. Dhawan, 'He was an actor for all seasons', *The Tribune*, 13 August 2000, http://www.tribuneindia.com/2000/20000813/ spectrum/main3.htm, accessed on 13 January 2016.

'*Zara kamzor ho gaya hoon.*'
  (I have grown weak.)

'*Nahin kamzor to nahin ho … tum to kabhi kamzor nahin they. Sirf duble ho gaye ho kuch.*'
  (No, you aren't weak … you were never weak. You have just lost some weight.)

These are the first lines exchanged when Aarti and JK meet after a gap of nine years. She corrects him on how he describes himself. Aarti talks about one of the most intrinsic qualities of her husband in a subtle way – the difference between '*kamzor*' (weak) and '*duble*' (having lost weight). Inspite of all their differences that led them to part ways, there is an inherent respect for each other. By bringing out the difference between the two words, Gulzar sums up JK's personality too. This leads to another aspect of the film: the character of JK is created and viewed largely through the prismatic lens of his wife.

Later, in one of the flashback scenes, when we find her discussing JK with her father, she tells him how playful he his – '*Bachche nahin hain, lekin bachpana bahut hai*' (he is not a child, but very childish) – as the conversation continues, we see the innocence of the male protagonist in his layered personality. Those lines are in response to the accusation by Aarti's father, Mr Bose, who asks her if JK is a child given the amount of time she spends taking care of him. There is another scene, when JK, unsuccessful in trying to put a drawstring in his pyjama, comes to Aarti to seek her help; his innocence and the endearing relationship between the two shine through in such moments.

JK is also a poet, to which Aarti says, '*Agar tum shayar nahin hote, to bahut ordinary hote*' (You would have been a very ordinary person, had you not been a poet). Her words bring forth two fascinating aspects of JK's personality. The first is the obvious – that he is a poet. The second is that he is also an ordinary man, a description which JK accepts. In a scene, where he and Aarti are quarrelling over a trivial domestic issue, he too admits it: '*Main ek seedha saada sa aadmi hoon aur hamesha rehna chahta hoon*' (I am an ordinary man and wish to remain this way).

Another distinct quality that is apparent is that JK is a man who has self-respect, and the line between self-respect and ego gets thinner and nearly blurs as the story progresses. When Aarti asks him to quit his job as a hotel manager and take up a better job using her father's recommendation or start his own business, JK not only dislikes the idea but loses his temper and tells his wife in black and white that if she has a problem being known as a hotel manager's wife, she could leave him; he would not hold her back.

It will not be incorrect to say that JK is just a simple man with a typical male ego. At one moment, he claims he loves his wife abundantly, at another, he makes a sexist, regressive comment: '*Mera shauhar banne ki koshish mat karo. Biwi ho, biwi ki jagah raho*' (Don't try to become my husband. You are a wife, remain so). This line alone portrays JK in a very different light. He had made it very clear that he wished to have a woman who stays at home, looks after him and takes care of the family. He isn't happy with Aarti's daily meetings and tells her categorically that he had spelt out even before the marriage itself that he would not be comfortable with a working woman. In many ways, this becomes the tipping point of their marriage. However, when the film ends, he is a different man – Aarti is hesitant going to work, but he tells her to go ahead and finish the task that she had undertaken. '*Main tumhe haara nahin dekhna chahta, na ghar mein, na bahar*' (I don't want to see you losing, neither at home, nor in the world outside).

Rehman (1921–1984)

Born in Lahore, Rehman migrated towards what is now India much before Partition and studied to be a pilot. However, having grown a dislike for the profession, he decided to try his luck in the film industry. Starting his career with *Shahjehan* in 1946, Rehman went on to act in an array of films, essaying a number of memorable roles. His most notable films are *Badi Behen* (1949), *Pyaasa* (1957), *Chaudvin ka Chand* (1960), *Sahib Bibi Aur Ghulam*

(1962), *Mere Mehboob* (1963), *Waqt* (1965), *Dil Ne Phir Yaad Kiya* (1966) among others. He was largely known to play sophisticated and suave characters, and even today is remembered for his dapper sense of style and grooming, and his dialogue delivery. No matter how small his role, it always left an impact, as was in the case of *Aandhi*.

Rehman as Mr K. Bose

As Aarti's father, Rehman's was a character then rarely seen in Hindustani cinema. He played the role of a businessman who has high hopes and aspirations for his daughter, and is upset that she wishes to marry and settle down. He tells her point-blank that her education, a degree in law, will prove to be a sheer waste if she, like other women, gets married and has children. A monologue delivered by him, opens up many layers of his personality:

> '*Shaadi karni hai! Kyun? Itni jaldi kya hai? Kya ho jayega shaadi se? Kaho kaho … samjhao mujhe … jahan tak main samjhta hoon, humare mulk mein takreeban athatis hazaar shaadiyan roz hotee hain … ismein se ek shaadi tumhari bhi hogee … phir, aage kya … future ka kya hoga? Humare yahan jo bartan manjhne wali aati hai, usne bhi shaadi ki hai … uske bachche bhi hain … tumhare bhi bachche ho jayenge. Lekin phir … phir kya? Kya yahi tumhari zindagi ka* goal *hai? Yahi tumhari* ambition *hai?* I am very much disappointed my

dear ... you just want to be one of these millions and millions of creatures ... *meri tumhare saath itni umeedein thi, main chahta tha ki tum bahut unchayee tak pahuncho ... lekin tum iss shaadi ki jaldi mein...*'

(You want to get married? Why? What is the hurry? What will you gain? Tell me ... make me understand ... as far as I know, twenty-eight thousand marriages take place every year in our country ... yours will be one of those ... Then? What next? What will happen to your future? The woman who comes to do our dishes ... she has also married ... she too has children ... you will also have children ... then what? Is that your goal for life? Is this your ambition? I am very disappointed my dear ... you just want to be one of these millions and millions of creatures ... I had such hopes from you ... I had wished to see you soar to great heights ... but in this hurry to get married, you...)

Much later, in one of the scenes, after Aarti is married, he scolds her for arriving late to a party meeting and missing out on important discussions. He looks disgusted when he tells him that she got late because she had to prepare and serve breakfast to JK and send him off to work. He even questions her if Brinda (their help) wasn't home, as she had to do the household chores. When Aarti says that she herself had to look after JK's breakfast, he comments, sarcastically,

'Kya haath se khilana padta hai?' (Do you have to feed him with your own hands?)

Mr Bose is never seen alone in the film. His character and personality comes through his conversations with his daughter. Though there are only a couple of scenes with him in the film, they are strong enough to drive home his authoritative and formidable personality.

A.K. Hangal (1914–2012)

A.K. Hangal was a freedom fighter and even spent three years in jail during British rule. It was his love for theatre that made him join IPTA. He later joined films when he was fifty, his first being *Teesri Kasam*. Although he always did cameos, he did leave an impression. The films that he is most remembered for are *Heer Ranjha* (1970), *Guddi* (1971), *Bawarchi* (1972), *Namak Haram* (1973), *Sholay* (1975), *Chitchor* (1976), *Shaukeen (1982)* and *Lagaan* (2001) among others.

Hangal as Brinda Kaka

Brinda Kaka is more than just a domestic help in the house. He appeals to Aarti to save her marriage. In one scene, where JK storms out of the house after an argument without having his breakfast, Brinda tells Aarti that a quarrel every morning isn't good for any relationship. He adds: *'Pati ki ichcha mein hee tumhari ichcha honi chahiye'* (The husband's wish should be your wish too). This does not go down very well with Aarti, who retorts, *'Pati hai na, koi* boss *to nahin. Koi naukar to nahin hoon ki unki marzi se nahin chaloongi to nikaal denge mujhe. Tumhari jagah hotee to yeh shayad darr hota mujhe'* (He is a husband and not a boss. I am not a servant that he would kick me out of a job if I don't do as told. Had I been in your place, I would perhaps have been scared).

Being referred to as a 'servant' pinches Brinda and he tries to tell Aarti that he wasn't in their house for work but for his love for her, and that she too did not have the right to throw him out. He had left her father's house after Aarti had married JK and had come with her. Aarti too realizes she had made a mistake the moment she had referred to Brinda as a servant. Brinda, however, fights tears and tells her that he would leave only when he alone wishes, not when anyone else wants. He says that once Mannu (JK and Aarti's daughter) grows up and gets married, he would go with her.

Brinda Kaka is also a key witness to the trajectory JK and Aarti's marital relationship takes – their marriage and initial love, their differences, arguments and finally, their separation. He feels helpless – though in his own ways, he tries to advise Aarti about the right thing to do.

Nine years later, when he sees Aarti, now a famous politician, he isn't sure how he must address her and is tongue-tied. However, this initial hesitation is put to rest as soon as Aarti touches his feet, catching him by surprise. After this meeting, when Aarti starts coming regularly to the bungalow to meet JK, she once confesses to Brinda Kaka that she has lost everything she had, to which he replies: *'Woh rishta hee kya jo haath chootne se choot jaye?'* (What kind of a relationship is that which is left behind when the two leave each other?)

Such is his wisdom and understanding of relationships.

Om Prakash (1919–1998) and Om Shivpuri (1938–1990)

Om Prakash started his career with All India Radio under the name of Fatehdin. Although he was very popular there, he left it to join films. His first film was *Dasi* (1944) and then *Dhamki* (1945) in Lahore. However, he migrated to India after Partition. After the initial days of struggle, he restarted his career in Hindustani cinema and then there was no looking back – he acted in about three hundred films. Some of his well-known films are *Zanjeer* (1973), *Chupke Chupke* (1975), *Julie* (1975), *Gol Maal* (1979), *Laawaris* (1981), *Namak Halal* (1982) and *Sharaabi* (1984) among others. He even produced a couple of films.

A veteran at the National School of Drama, Om Shivpuri later started the theatre group 'Dishantar' and finally joined films. His first film was *Ashad ka Ek Din* (1971), followed by *Koshish* (1972). His other prominent films were *Sholay* (1975), *Mausam* (1975), *Kitaab* (1977), *Don* (1978), *Meera* (1979), *Insaaf ka Taraazu* (1980), *Naseeb* (1981), *Arth* (1982), and *Coolie* (1983) among others.

Om Prakash as Lallu Laal and Om Shivpuri as Chander Sen

Lallu Laal and Chander Sen are the mouthpiece representing the filmmaker's take on the political scene of the country. Both characters are shown conniving and strategizing methods to win the elections. Not surprisingly, they adopt dubious ways to achieve their goal. If Lallu Laal is a worker in Aarti's party, Chander Sen is the leader of the opposition. Both are shown to be unscrupulous, forever plotting against the opposite party. They even instigate the common man and lead the ordinary public towards violence.

When Aarti Devi is hurt, Lallu Laal doesn't call the doctor – he wants the press and photographers to reach there first. He intends to make full use of the situation and turn this episode in the party's favour. It is the crafty Lallu Laal's plan to provoke Agarwal to stand for the elections since if he does so, the votes of the mill workers would go to him and not to Chander Sen.

This issue of dividing the vote bank is explicitly spelt out, as Lallu Laal explains the same to another party worker:

'*Ek tareeqa hai Chander Sen ki taaqat todne ka. Woh yeh … ki Agarwal ko election mein khada kar diya jaye.*'
(There is one way to defeat the rising power of Chander Sen. Make Agarwal contest the elections.)

'*Usse fayda?*' (What use would that be of?)

'*Yeh jo dus aadmi ek jagah hain, unhe jeetne ke liye tumhe kitne vote chahiye?*' (How many votes do you need to win against ten people?)

'*Gyarah.*' (Eleven.)

'*Agar main inhe paanch paanch mein batwa doon … phir?*' (If I divide them in five each … then?)

'*Chhaih.*' (Six.)

This plan is hatched without Aarti Devi's knowledge. As expected, when Chander Sen gets to know of Agarwal contesting the elections, he is visibly perturbed since he is aware that the votes of the mill workers would go to him. However, the tables turn when he gets to know that there is a strike in his mill. After giving it some thought, he strategizes and conveys the plan to his party workers.

'*Mazdooron ko bhadkaye rakhkho aur kisi tarah ka koi samjhauta mat hone do.*' (Keep the workers on edge and make sure that no compromise can take place.)

The scene that follows is that of workers protesting in front of Agarwal Mills, and Lallu Laal is seen standing at the back, looking complacent and satisfied that the plan has worked in his favour. As we go deeper into the story, the politics gets dirtier and murkier. When Chander Sen gets the whiff of a relationship between Aarti and JK, he acquires proof in the form of photographs and it is with this information that he launches his newspaper, *Zamana*, maligning his political opponent.

'*Geeta haath mein le kar jung nahin ladi jaa sakti. Bhagwan Krishna nahin lad sake to yeh kya ladegi.*' (You can't fight war with Geeta in your hands. If Lord Krishna couldn't, how would she?)

Again, it is Lallu Laal, who at one of Agarwal's speeches, hands over eggs wrapped in ten-rupee notes to the audiences, asking them to keep the money and throw the eggs at the podium.

Gulzar has used both these characters to strengthen the background of the film, and they are instrumental in conveying the inherent message. While he showcased dirty politics through Lallu Laal and Chander Sen, he has also provided Aarti Devi as the character who could counter their points of view and practices.

Gulzar's characters are always carved out well. *Aandhi*'s are no different. They aren't static in their perspectives and their personalities change as the story develops. We witness a definite shift in the patriarchal mindsets. We see the transfer of power from the men in the film to the only woman in the script. Aarti's father tries to persuade her and even dictate terms with regard to how she should lead her life. Later, her husband JK too demands that he wants an ordinary wife who would look after the house and the family.

However, in the course of the film, we notice Aarti taking decisions for herself. She goes to meet the husband in the 'dark', knowing that it might not be good for her political ambitions, but she listens to her heart. There is a change in the male protagonist also. The same JK, who was very adamant that his wife shouldn't work, now encourages her to go ahead and live her dream.

chapter four

The Poetry

☙

Songs have a unique place in Indian culture. Be it the morning bhajans and azans, to the tunes the milkman and the newspaperwala arriving at our doorsteps whistle, to what we hum while performing all the household chores, to the lullabies we sing to our children at night – there is a place for poetry and music in all facets of our everyday life. India has a very interesting grounding historically for various forms of songs and poetry, be it through oral narratives or through folk traditions. If there are harvest songs, there are also those meant not only for joyous occasions like weddings, but also for mourning. Any cultural or religious activity in India is replete with poetry and music.

This is the reason why music and poetry have been an integral part of the Hindustani film industry right from the beginning. *Alam Ara* (1931), the first talkie, had seven songs, but *Shirin Farhad* (1932) was a musical, and *Indrasabha*, which released the same year had seventy-two songs, as forms of verses woven into the narrative! It was in 1935 that Nitin Bose and his brother Mukul Bose along with music composer R.C. Boral introduced pre-recorded singing. This was a major landmark for Hindustani cinema. However, the songs still remained based in folklore from Bengal, Maharashtra and Punjab. It was nearly after a decade that the classical forms crept in. Consequently, as the Hindustani film industry developed, so did the music industry. One could see the growth and Western influence, especially of pop and rock music, become more obvious and prominent. As Ashok Da. Ranade says, 'The films became prominent in liberating film music from the grip of music rooted in "classical" musical traditions – whether religion oriented or theatre-influenced.'[29]

With each passing year, the importance of songs in Hindustani cinema increased and in 1949, for the first time, songs were not only recorded but also released as LPs for consumption before the films premiered.[30] Lalitha Gopalan in the essay, 'Hum Aapke Hain Koun? – Cinephilia and Indian Films' writes of the importance of songs and dance sequences in Indian films and how in the early years of

---

29 A. Ranade, *Hindi Film Song: Music Beyond Boundaries*, New Delhi and Chicago: Promilla & Co. Publishers, 2006, p. 124.
30 Ibid., p. 128.

Indian cinema, songs were a key component in helping to promote the film.[31] This holds true even today, as the music gets released before the film's release, with the aim to cash in on the latter's popularity.

It is also true that songs in Hindustani cinema are criticized for just 'being there' and not providing any value addition to the core story. However, this is not the case with *Aandhi*. The music of the film had the opposite effect: *Aandhi* is remembered for its songs.

Anil Zankar, in *Mughal-e-Azam: Legend as Epic*, writes: 'For songs to be an integral part of the film narrative, they have to be an essential and well-defined part of the script.'[32] This description holds completely true for *Aandhi*.

Undoubtedly, *Aandhi*'s music is its strength and proves that one cannot deny the importance of music in Indian cinema. Meghnad Desai says, 'Music is almost unfailingly the key to any Hindustani film being a hit or not … the golden era of film melodies, the 1950s, was full of films with no storyline to speak of, or any pretensions to cinematic excellence, just a handful of evergreen numbers around which the protagonists sang and danced.'[33] For *Aandhi*,

---

31 Eleftheriotis and Needlam (eds), *Asian Cinemas*, p. 333.

32 Anil Zankar, *Mughal-e-Azam: Legend as an Epic*, New Delhi: HarperCollins Publishers, 2013, p. 126..

33 M. Desai, *Pakeezah: An Ode to A Bygone World*, New Delhi, HarperCollins Publishers, 2013, p. 132.

Gulzar roped in R.D. Burman, with whom he already had a successful association. Burman, also known as Pancham, brought about a change to Hindustani cinema at a time when it was most desired. The Gulzar–RD partnership is noteworthy on several counts.

The first film that they did together was *Parichay*. They complemented each other's talents very well and went on to create magic in several films, namely *Ijaazat, Parichay, Kinara, Khushboo, Namkeen, Kitaab, Angoor, Libaas, Doosri Sita, Basera, Jeeva, Sitara, Ghar, Masoom, Devata, Khubsoorat* and *Gol Maal* among many others.

Pancham began his career when he assisted his father, music composer S.D. Burman, in *Chhote Nawab* (1961). Ganesh Anantharaman, in *Bollywood Melodies: A History of Hindi Film Songs*, talks of this change that R.D. Burman brought about: 'He most successfully Indianized pop and jazz for Hindi films.'[34] Anantharaman adds, 'If Pankaj Mullick brought Rabindra Sangeet into films, Naushad Hindustani classical, Madan Mohan ghazals, [then] R.D. Burman pop and jazz.'[35] This was the beginning of his career when he gave hits like '*Aaja aaja, main hoon pyar tera*' (Come to me, I am your love) for *Teesri Manzil* (1966), '*Piya tu, ab to aaja*' (You are my love, oh do come to me) for

---

34 G. Anantharaman, *Bollywood Melodies: A History of Hindi Film Song*, New Delhi: Penguin Books, 2008, p. 66.

35 Ibid., p. 21.

Caravan (1971) and '*Dum maro dum*' (Take a puff) for *Hare Rama Hare Krishna* (1971). Such music shaped his image and the masses would associate songs that rhythm, pop and jazz with R.D. Burman. But it was the same person who also gave music to films like *Amar Prem* (1972), *Ghar* (1978), *Gol Maal* (1979) *and Khoobsurat* (1980), where the songs were slow-paced and mellow. His soundtrack for *Padosan* (1968) needs a special mention as the variety he brought in for songs like '*Kehna hai*' (I have to express), '*Mere saamne wali khidki mein*' (In the window opposite my house), '*Ek chatur naar*' (A cunning man) and '*Meri pyari Bindu*' (My dear Bindu), seamlessly blend classical with contemporary music. Anantharaman wrote, 'It was only in Gulzar's films that RD managed to bridge the dichotomy between class appeal and mass adulation ... such was the tuning between the two that they often instinctively understood what the other wanted. Hence, RD could soar high without any constraints...'[36]

Anirudha Bhattacharjee and Balaji Vittal, in their book *R.D. Burman: The Man, The Music*, write that the music of *Aandhi* 'is the result of a symbiosis of the best of both Pancham's and Gulzar's worlds'.[37] Many a time, it is the combination of the poet and the music director that does

---

36 Ibid., p. 69.

37 A. Bhattacharjee and B. Vittal, *R.D. Burman: The Man, The Music*, New Delhi: HarperCollins Publishers, 2011, p. 155.

wonders, writes Ashok Da. Ranade in his book *Hindi Film Song: Music Beyond Boundaries*: 'His duets for Lata and compositions for Gulzar's lyrics stand out as a representative of a mastery of a musical idiom which was essentially tender.'[38] These words sum up R.D. Burman's craftsmanship in *Aandhi*.

The film had three romantic songs and a qawwali which was a satire on the political situation of the country and the attitude that its politicians had towards the nation.[39] The songs too, are as finely structured as the screenplay, and depict Gulzar's skills and craftsmanship. Each song takes us deep inside the characters' emotions and inner turmoil and it is this quality that elevates these songs from being mere 'fillers' in the story. Even though *Aandhi* is a film involving themes of politics, love and the changing nature of relationships, it is its songs that bind the film together, filling up all cinematic gaps to ensure a seamless narrative. All the four songs of the film were successful in creating the emotional intensity that the story demanded and Gulzar desired.

The three romantic songs of the film, sung by Lata Mangeshkar and Kishore Kumar, portray three different stages in the life of the couple and their complex relationship. If *'Iss mod se jaate hain'* (We cross this path)

---

38 Ibid., p. 305.
39 See Appendix I for the lyrics of the songs.

is at the beginning of their courtship, '*Tum aa gaye ho, noor aa gaya hai*' (Your arrival has brightened my life) is when they have moved to the next stage of romance and are contemplating marriage. And finally, '*Tere bina zindagi se koi shikva to nahin*' (There is no complaint in life, except [about] you) is when they meet after nine years. There is a connect between the three romantic songs as there is a recurrent metaphor of travelling in them.

Iss mod se jaate hain…

The song '*Iss mod se jaate hain*' is a song in flashback, a storytelling device typical of Gulzar. Another characteristic of the poet is the unusual use of words, and their clever juxtaposition to encourage imagery as in the line '*Kuch sust qadam raste, kuch tez qadam raahein*' (Some lazy ways, some quick routes).

Shot in the picturesque locales of Kashmir where the green pastures overshadow the rest of the scenery, this song starts with a shot of the mountain peaks, showing the pinnacle of their love, the sunlight through the trees depicting the happy future that the lovers expect for themselves, and a gushing stream portraying the flow of the emotions. In the lines '*Aandhi ki tarah ud kar, ek raah guzarti hai*' (Flying like the wind, a path runs), Gulzar has used the metaphor of *aandhi* (storm) to suggest that sometimes the road ahead is chosen by destiny, and sometimes by other factors.

The song continues with the line, '*In reshami rahon mein, ek raah woh hogee, tum tak jo pahunchi hai*' (Among these silky paths, there would be one which would lead to you) continuing its emphasis on the imagery of pathways and routes, underscoring the metaphor of travel and the sense of movement within a relationship. In '*Yeh soch ke baithi hoon*' (I sit, wondering), again the mention of 'baithi' (literally meaning 'sitting', although here it is meant in the sense of pausing or waiting) indicates that in the midst of the journey, there is a need for pause too, to reflect and think of love and a happy life.

It is a positive song about the promise of fulfilment of love. However, the first two lines of the song are repeated once again in the last frame of the film where JK bids adieu to Aarti and the latter leaves. The hesitant Aarti steps aboard a helicopter and it is JK, firm but with a heavy heart, who helps her board the chopper and closes the door. The film ends with these lines as the helicopter flies away and JK keeps looking at it.

Tum aa gaye ho, noor aa gaya hai...

Picturized admist flowers, mainly roses and dahlias in full bloom, the setting of the song is symbolic of the blossoming of love between the couple. The soaring bird in the sky, described in the very first stanza, is a reference to the soaring passion of young love and its desire to break free and fly away together.

The fountain shown at the beginning isn't turned on, but when it spurts open, it symbolizes the outburst of emotions. Even the structure in the background of this garden is not in ruins, showing more strength and positivity of the situation.

The line, *Din dooba nahin, raat doobi nahin, jaane kaisa hai safar* (Neither has the day set, nor the night, wonder what this journey is like), although mentioning the night, emphasizes on its continuity, merging with the day. The word *safar* (journey), brings in the metaphor travelling yet again. Also, the line *kahan se chale, kahan ke liya* (From where had I started, where was I headed) continues with the recurring image.

Tere bina zindagi se koi, shikva to nahin...

When the song, '*Tere bina zindagi se koi, shikva to nahin*' plays in the background, the meaningful glances of longing shared between Aarti and JK show the deep love they once had for each other. The song begins with the couple walking together on a full-moon night in the ruins of Mattan in Kashmir. These ruins are a metaphor for their own relationship: strong, once upon a time, but now a casualty of the winds of change and the passing of time. Initially, Aarti is seen just looking at JK and following him, with the song playing in the background. The fact that she still yearns for him is visible in her tear-laden eyes. She does not, however, shed any. The first stanza of the song is in the woman's voice, emphasizing that it's possibly the woman who is more regretful of the way things stand. The song is an ode to the years gone by, wasted away by their separation. Remnants of affection are also apparent, when JK, feeling the chill in the air, offers his own coat to Aarti. The line 'Kaash aisa ho tere qadmon se chunke manzil chalein, aur kahin, door kahin' (If only, the route touched your feet and went, to some faraway land) has been picturized on the steps where the couple sit down to pause and introspect. It is JK who holds Aarti's hand and makes her sit. She too holds his palms in hers and the feeling of repentance and regret is apparent. The lines continue about the longing for the manzil, the destination and is intercepted by dialogue:

JK: 'Suno Aarti, yeh jo phoolon ki belein nazar aa rahi hain, darasal yeh belein nahin hain. Arbi mein aayatein likhin hain. Isse din ke waqt dekhna chahiye. Bilkul saaf nazar aati hain. Din ke waqt, ye sara paani se bhara rahta hai. Din ke waqt jab yeh phuwarre...'

(Aarti, these flower vines that you see aren't actually vines. These are verses written in Arabic. One should see them in daylight. They appear very clear. During the day, all of it is filled with water. During the day, when these fountains...)

Aarti: 'Rehne do. Kahan aa paungi din ke waqt?'

(Let it be. How will I be able to come during the day?)

69

JK: '*Yeh jo chaand hai na, isse raat ke waqt dekhna. Yeh din mein nahin nikalta.*' (Both laugh)

(This moon, regard it only at night. It doesn't come out in the day.)

Aarti: '*Yeh to roz nikalta hoga.*'

(This must be visible every day.)

JK: '*Haan. Lekin beech mein amawas aa jati hai. Waise to amawas pandrah din ki hotee hai, lekin is baar bahut lambi thi.*'

(Yes. Though the moonless night comes after every fifteen days, this time it lasted for a very long time.)

Aarti (with tears in her eyes): '*Nau baras lambi thi na?*'

(Wasn't it nine years long?)

One notices subtle humour in the dialogue when JK refers to the moon coming out only at night. It is following these lines that Aarti expresses her desire to keep on crying, buried in his arms and even adds that she feels that there are tears in JK's eyes as well. Only then does the song continue with the male voice. The oft-used image of the moon, rather the favourite image of Gulzar, which he himself claims that he has a 'copyright' on, comes again in the song with the line – '*Tum jo kah do to, aaj ki raat, chaand doobega nahin, raat ko rok lo*' (Only if you say, the moon will not set, do stop the night).

The desire that time stops is apparent in the misty eyes of the couple. The two of them visit the ruins every night, strengthening the bond they once severed. The relationship seems to mend as Aarti eventually puts her head on JK's shoulder and weeps, thinking about the lost years.

In *R.D. Burman*, Bhattacharjee and Vittal write that this song continues to be immensely popular. 'The monumental success of the song can be gauged by the response it gets even today. The number of views on YouTube is around 3.5 million, definitely the highest for any Hindi film song considered "retro", and probably highest among all Hindi film songs.'[40]

Salaam kijeye, aali janab aayein hain...

The fourth song of the film is a qawwali, an effective satire, where Gulzar's lyrics poke fun at the intentions of politicians and points out the stark differences in their attitude before and after elections. This song is successful in bringing forth Gulzar's own opinions and ideas about the political ruling class. What he didn't try to express through dialogue, he did through verse and its themes and message continue to

---

40 Bhattacharjee and Vittal, *R.D. Burman*, p. 156.

be relevant even today. Like most qawwalis, this too begins with an interlude of verses thematically adjoined to the rest of the song, though these words do not feature in the verses that follow. Here the words are: '*Aarti man maanti, kehna kyun nahin maanti, paathshaala mein chhutti ho gayee, basta kyun nahin baandhti?*' (O stubborn Aarti, why don't you listen, the school has shut down, why don't you pack your bag?) and the song continues as '*Salaam kijiye, aali janaab aaye hain*' (Pay your respects, Her Majesty is here). Accompanied by the traditional harmonium and the characteristic clapping that complements a qawwali, the song deviates from being a praise – all qawwalis originally were words of praise – and is a complete satire.

Interestingly, there are cutouts of a chair, hanging from trees, seen at three different points in the song. Chairs seem to be the symbol of the opposition party, as during the credit rolls, where there is a backdrop of the elections, many jeeps are seen with cutouts of chairs on them. One can interpret the chair as a well-known symbol of the power that politicians long for. Who occupies those chairs is a decision that rests with the common man and the votes they cast.

As the song progresses, there are two long queues in the backdrop. The first is outside the government ration shop. The second one is for water, where men, women and children are seen in line, with buckets, waiting at a common tap. The emphasis is on how the common man is queuing up for the basic needs and daily commodities. Elections come and go, political parties change, but the problems and the issues of the common man remain the same. We then move on to half-built houses, symbolic of half-baked promises by politicians. These houses under construction suggest that the common man is finally aware. The words, '*Humaare* vote *kharidenge humko ann dekar, yeh nange jism chupa dete hain qafan dekar* (They want to buy our votes, giving us some grains, they cover our bodies, giving us shrouds), clearly indicate that the common man is not only aware of politicians' intentions but also not willing to take things lying down.

The song ends with heightened optimism: 'Vote *denge magar abke yon nahin denge, chunaav aane do hum aapse nipat lenge*' (We will vote, but not like this, let the elections come, we will settle scores) coupled with sarcasm and satire when an old man laughingly adds, '*Yeh inqalaab layen hain*' (They have brought about a revolution).

There is another interesting point involving the lyrics. The male protagonist of the film, JK, is a poet too and at two instances he talks about a poem that he has written. Once during his and Aarti's courtship, JK recites this over the phone:

'*Aao tumko utha loon kandhon par*
Tum uchchak kar shareer hothon se
Choom lena yeh chaand ka maatha

Aaj ki raat dekha na tumne
Kaise chup chup ke kohniyon ke bal
Chaand itna kareeb aaya hai'

(Come, let me lift you on my shoulders
You can soar, and with your mischievous lips
Kiss the moon's forehead.
Tonight, you haven't noticed,
How silently, on its elbows
The moon has come so close.)

It comes as no surprise that when the filmmaker is Gulzar, the actor-poet will write a poem in which the central image will be that of a moon.

The second incident where a poem is mentioned in the film is when Aarti and JK are married and he wishes to recite one to her, but is unable to do so after her witty response. All the same, there is a mention that he has penned down a poem.

With three utterly romantic songs, a poem and a political-satirical qawwali, Gulzar mapped the film with magnificient verse. As film poetry and songs are a crucial part of Hindustani cinema, *Aandhi* can be considered to be a perfect example of intellectually stimulating cinema marrying mass appeal through poetry.

chapter five

The Language

CR

Ravi Vasudevan, in the essay 'Addressing the Spectator of a "Third World" National Cinema', emphasizes the fact that the 'language of Bombay cinema is Hindustani'.[41] Like all arts, the language of the films also represents the lingo of the times. If one traces the language of the films from the 1940s to the present day, there is a stark difference thanks to the changing nature of language. Art and cinema imitate life, and vice versa. The language of the common people seeps into cinema as well.

For a film by Gulzar, even an entire chapter on language isn't enough. A wordsmith unlike none other, he knows how to play with words. In this chapter, there are two aspects that have been looked into, and analysed – one, his

---

41 Eleftheriotis and Needlam (eds) *Asian Cinemas*, p. 310.

choice of words, and two, the subtle touches of humour he has employed to great effect in a fairly serious film.

Choice of words

The characteristic use and the style of Gulzar's writing comes out very prominently in this film. The opening lines of the film are:

> '*Yakeen maniye, mujhe koi shauk nahin hai election ladne ka. Aur na hee kisi doctor ne kaha hai ki main election ladoon. Lekin mujhe election ladna padta hai. Apne huqooq ke liye. Janta ke huqook ke liye.*'
>
> (Believe me, I have no desire to fight the elections. Neither has any doctor asked me to. But I have to fight the elections – for my own rights, for the rights of the common man.)

One could note the choice of the Urdu words with elements of a conversational tone blending beautifully. Also, the first dialogue that Aarti Devi delivers when she addresses her party workers, asking them to be seated, is 'Sit down' instead of its Hindustani equivalent. Her choice of words draws from her characterization. Her dialogues are peppered with English throughout the film, especially when she is in the comfort of her personal zone. When a staff member from Hotel Aashiyana welcomes her with a basket of flowers, she addresses him in English, a language she can speak effortlessly. It's wedded to her character.

When she reaches Allahabad and looks at a poster designed for the political rally, Aarti Devi points out that it has too much use of English and should instead have Hindi. It is interesting to note that she makes this remark in English: 'English *zyada lag rahi hai*. They should be more in Hindi.' (There is too much of English. They should be more in Hindi). Further, it is worth noting that although the banner says 'Vote for Aarti Devi', the script on the banner is Devnagari. This style is a conscious effort from Gulzar. India, being a country of many languages and, therefore, many scripts, has always found the debate around the national language a bit sensitive. Mahatma Gandhi was a strong advocate of Hindustani and preferred it as the national language of free India, instead of Hindi. His idea was to bridge the difference between Hindi and Urdu, languages which had by then begun to be associated with religions – Hinduism and Islam respectively. Gandhi had even tried initiating the idea of a common script. Considering the widespread illiteracy amongst the masses, he believed a common, neutral script would bridge the gap between both religions and help everyone start on a clean slate. However, things did not turn out the way as he saw it.

In time, the rift between the two languages only increased – Hindi went on to become more and more

Sanskritized and Urdu more Persianized. Today, one gets to hear this Sanskritized Hindi through All India Radio and Doordarshan, both state-owned broadcasters. Similarly, the Persianized Urdu is broadcast on Urdu channels. However, the language of the masses is Hindustani and that is the language Gulzar used in the film. It was a conscious choice to do so.

The title of the film, *Aandhi* and the symbol of Aarti's party, *panchhi* (bird) are two words with which Gulzar plays with, at different levels. One interpretation of the title is the tumultuous relationship between Aarti and JK. Another interpretation is that of the storm brewing in the political cauldron of the nation. When Lallu Laal gets a whiff of some sort of a relationship between Aarti Devi and JK, he comments: '*Aandhi aayegi, aandhi*' (A storm will come, a storm).

He seems to confirm the forthcoming prediction. Further, in an interesting play of words around the election symbol of Aarti Devi's party: *panchhi*, Chander Sen, in his first speech in the film makes fun of it, saying:

'*Yeh panchhi kisi ke nahin hote! Yeh panchhi kisi ke nahin honge! Udd jayenge aapka daana, paani aur vote le kar aur jaa kar baithenge ... wahin kisi raajdhaani ki chowk par ... aur aapko hamesha hamesha ke liye bhooka pyaasa chhod jayenge.*'

(These birds are not loyal to anyone! They will never be loyal to anyone! Snatching away your share of food, they will fly away after getting your votes and will go and perch themselves in the capital ... leaving you all behind, hungry and starving.)

Lallu Laal's response is just the opposite. When JK confirms by asking him if the same Aarti Devi whose party symbol was *panchhi* is coming to his hotel to stay, Laal responds, saying: '*Aur kiska dam hai jo itna uncha udd sake aasman tak?*' (Who else has the strength to fly as high as to touch the sky?)

Gulzar also carefully chose the names of the two newspapers featured in the film. The first is 'Watan Press' – *watan* means 'country'. It is symbolic as the newspaper of the country, the mouthpiece of the masses. As the film unfolds, Chandra Sen also launches his newspaper and calls it 'Zamana Press' – loosely translated, it means 'newspaper of the times'. With this title, Sen tries to indicate that he – and his newspaper – are representing contemporary issues. The name of the hotel where JK was working was Aashiyana, meaning 'abode'. Although it was a hotel for Aarti, the politician, it turns into a sort of home for Aarti, the wife. She tries indulging in activities like making tea and even tries her hand at cooking just to feel the simple pleasures of being 'at home'.

Given the complicated nature of JK and Aarti's relationship, only a master of wordplay could handle their scenes with maturity. Given the awkwardness in the air when JK and Aarti suddenly meet after a gap of nine years, the dialogues required a lot to be conveyed using the bare minimum of words. For instance, in the scene where Aarti comments that JK's house is very tidy and clean, her intention is not so much to compliment him on the cleanliness; she only wants to know if there is now another woman in JK's life who is taking care of him and the house. One can see the sense of relief on her face when JK says that it is Brinda who takes care of the house. After a few moments, JK, speaking about himself, says, '*Kamzor ho gaya hoon*' (I have grown weak) to which his estranged wife responds, correcting him, '*Kamzor nahin ... tum kabhi kamzor nahin the ... duble ho gaye ho*' (Not weak ... you were never weak ... you have lost weight). This kind of mastery over words unpeels several layers of the film and its characters.

Another characteristic of Gulzar is his use of words from different languages and blending them beautifully. The word '*nasheman*' used in the song, '*Iss mod se jaate hain*' is a Persian word and means 'nest', or 'house'. There is an anecdote around this word: R.D. Burman, with his limited knowledge of Urdu poetry, was baffled by the song's lyrics and asked Gulzar, if *nasheman* was the name of a town.[42]

---

42 Bhattacharjee and Vittal, *R.D. Burman*, p. 155.

Humour

Aandhi deals with a serious subject and its theme isn't light in vein. But the screenplay has plenty of moments full of tender, clever humour. It is moments like these that actually reflect the kind of companionship and the affection JK and Aarti share. In the same scene, discussed above, she, trying to look elsewhere, asks him:

> Aarti – '*Yeh moochhein kab se rakhleen?*'
>   (Since when have you sported a moustache?)
> JK – '*Kuch saal pehle ... tumhe achhi nahin lagti thi na?*'
>   (It has been some years now ... You never liked them, isn't it?)
> Aarti (smiling) – '*Isi liye rakhleen?*'
>   (Is that why you have grown them?)
> JK (smiling) – '*Nahin, nahin ... aiwaein*'
>   (No, no – just like that.)

This word '*aiwaein*' seems innocuous but it is a throwback to the way the two characters used to speak with each other and the fond relationship they once shared. It is a peek at the threads they are trying to pick up from the point they had walked their separate ways. As the film does not move in a linear fashion and is sprinkled with flashbacks, in one such scene, the couple is shown in a jovial mood, when JK asks for her help in putting a drawstring in his pyjama.

JK – '*Bahut* try *kiya*. Sincerely try *kiya* ... *lekin yeh naada nahin pad raha.*'

(I tried a lot. With sincerity ... but am unable to put this drawstring in my pyjama.)

Aarti – '*Uffo – ek to aapke naade ne pareshaan kar rakha hai. Rassi pakad kar pahaad chadh jaate hain, lekin ek naada pyjame mein nahin daal pate.*'

(Uff ... for one, your drawstring troubles me a lot. You can climb a mountain with a rope, but can't put a drawstring in your pyjama.)

JK – '*Dekho, pahad chadhna aur pyjame mein naada daalna – yeh dono alag alag baatein hain. Hockey khelte hue main goal to kar sakta hoon lekin sui mein dhaaga nahin daal sakta. Iska matlab yeh nahin hua, ki main kuch nahin...*'

(Look here, these are two very different things – climbing a mountain and puting a drawstring in a pyjama. I can score a goal while playing hockey, but can't put thread in a needle. This doesn't mean that I am unable...)

Aarti – '*Kuch nahin kar sakte ... deejiye, pyjama deejiye.*'

(You can't do anything ... here ... give it to me ...)

JK – '*Dekho, yeh mat kehna ki mujhse kuch nahin ho sakta hai ... aisi kavita likh sakta hoon ki jhoom kar doobara shaadi karne ko tayyar ho jayogi. Sunaun?*'

(Look here, don't say that I can't do anything. I can write such a poem that you will be swept off your feet and marry me again. Will I recite?)

Aarti – '*Nahin ... mujhe aur bahut kaam hain.*'
(No ... I have loads to do.)

JK – '*Maslan? Aisa aur kaun sa kaam hai jo meri kavita se zyada* interesting *hai?*'
(For instance? What kind of work do you have that is more interesting than my poetry?)

Aarti – '*Yehi ... aapke pyjame mein naada daalna.*'
(This ... putting drawstrings in your pyjamas.)

JK – '*Kahan meri kavita aur kahan naada ... saari* image *kharaab kar ke rakh di.*'
(What a comparison! My poetry versus a drawstring! You have spoiled the entire imagery.)

This scene about putting the drawstring in pyjamas gives us a little peep into the lives of JK and Aarti. Interestingly, this conversation takes place in the kitchen, while she is working. JK's apologetic pleading that he had 'sincerely' tried to put the drawstring in his pyjama, Aarti's calling the act as more interesting than listening to his poetry, the little smile that she has on her face, as she pulls JK's leg – all of it along with wit and humour forms an integral part of their relationship.

It becomes apparent again when JK and Aarti have a discussion on naming their newly born daughter.

Aarti – '*Kuch naam socha hai?*'
  (Have you thought of a name?)

JK – '*Hmmm, Manorama.*'

Aarti – '*Chhi … uss moti ka khayal aata hai … mujhe achha nahin laga.*'
  (Chhi … I am reminded of that fat woman[43] … I don't like it)

JK – '*Poora naam thodi lekar bulaya karenge. Chhota sa bulayenge – Mann.*'
  (We won't call out the full name. We will call her – Mann.)

Aarti – '*Woh to bahut chhota hai.*'
  (That is too short.)

JK – '*Do baar bulayenge – Mann Mann.*'
  (We would call out twice – Mann Mann.)

---

43 The reference is to a character artist in Hindustani cinema, who was rather fat in appearance.

Aarti – '*Hunh … lagta hai koi ghantee baja raha hai.*'
(Seems like someone is ringing the bell.)

JK (laughing) – '*To phir … Mannu bulaya karenge.*'
(In that case, we will call her Mannu.)

This interaction then cuts to a scene where the daughter, Mannu is about three years old and is sitting of the floor playing with her toys, while JK is lying on his stomach on the sofa, with a paper and pen in his hand, and Brinda is pressing his shoulders and back. As Aarti comes to the room, clearing up the toys scattered all over, JK asks her to wait.

JK – '*Aarti, yeh suno … maine ek kavita likhi hai.*'
(Aarti, listen to this … I have written a poem.)

Aarti – '*Aap kavita likh rahe hain?*'
(Are you writing a poem?)

She bursts out laughing.

JK – '*Isme hansne ki kya baat hai?*'
(What is there to laugh about it?)

Aarti – '*Bilkul* toothpaste *ki* tube *lagte ho. Upar se Brinda kaka daba rahe hain, saamne se kavita nikal rahi hai.*'

(You resemble a toothpaste tube. Brinda kaka is pressing you from the back, and a poem is coming out from the front.)

Brinda also joins in, laughing. This blend of romance and humour brings out the fun-loving relationship the two once had. At yet another point, JK asks Aarti when she had last cooked, to which she replies, *jab main barah saal ki thi* and both burst out laughing. This was Aarti's way of making fun of JK as he claimed to have done everything, right from reciting poetry at mushairas or even facing a bullet for a revolution, at the age of 12!

While concluding this chapter, one can't help but quote the scene where Aarti, drunk, meets JK. It is a classic example of how Gulzar chooses his words and blends humour in it. JK uses the word '*antaghafeel*' to describe Aarti's inebriated state. It is rather difficult to look for an apt translation for it in English; 'drunk' just doesn't cut it. As JK himself elaborates on the word with '*batti gul*' (light switched off), implying that one is not in his/her senses. Without complicating much, a lot is said using an economy of words and keeping the subtle humour intact.

Appendix I

The Songs

☙

(1)

Tum aa gaye ho, noor aa gaya hai... (2)
Nahi to, charaagon se, lau jaa rahi thi
Jeene ki tumse, wajeh mil gayi hai
Badi bewajeh, zindagi, jaa rahi thi
Tum aa gaye ho, noor aa gaya hai

Kaha se chale, kaha ke liye, ye khabar nahi thi magar
Koi bhi seera, jaha jaa mila, wahi tum miloge
Ke ham tak tumhaari duwa aa rahi thi
Tum aa gaye ho, noor aa gaya hai
Nahi to, charaagon se, lau jaa rahi thi
Tum aa gaye ho, noor aa gaya hai

Din dooba nahi, raat doobi nahi, jaane kaisa hai safar
Khwaabo ke diye, aankho mein liye, wahi aa rahe the
Jaha se tumhaari sada aa rahi thi
Tum aa gaye ho, noor aa gaya hai
Nahi to, charaagon se, lau jaa rahi thi
Tum aa gaye ho, noor aa gaya hai

(2)

Iss mod se jaate hain... (2)
Kuchh sust qadam raste, kuchh tez qadam raahe... (2)
Patthar ki haveli ko, shishe ke gharaundo mein
Tinko ke nasheman tak, iss mod se jaate hain
Aaa ... is mod se jaate hain

Aandhi ki tarha ud kar, ik raah guzarti hai... (2)
Sharmaati huwi koi, qadmo se utarti hai
In reshmi raaho mein, ik raah to woh hogi
Tum tak jo pahonchti hai, iss mod se jaati hai
Iss mod se jaate hain

Ik door se aati hai, paas aake palat-ti hai... (2)
Ik raah akeli si, ruktii hai na chalti hai
Ye soch ke baithhi hoon, ik raah to woh hogi
Tum tak jo pahonchti hai, iss mod se jaati hai
Iss mod se jaate hain... (2)
Kuchh sust qadam raste, kuchh tez qadam raahe
Patthar ki haveli ko, shishe ke gharaundo mein

Tinko ke nasheman tak, iss mod se jaate hain
Aaa ... iss mod se jaate hain

(3)

Tere bina zindagi se koi, shikva, to nahi, shikva nahi, shikva
nahi, shikva nahi
Tere bina zindagi bhi lekin, zindagi, to nahi, zindagi nahi,
zindagi nahi, zindagi nahi
Tere bina zindagi se, shikva, to nahi

Kaash aisa ho tere qadmo se, chun ke manzil chale, aur kahi
door kahi... (2)
Tum gar saath ho, manzilo ki, kami to nahi
Tere bina zindagi se koi, shikva, to nahi

Jee mein aata hai, tere daaman mein, sar jhuka ke hum rote rahe,
rote rahe... (2)
Teri bhi aankho mein, aansuo ki, nami to nahi

Tere bina zindagi se koi, shikva, to nahi,
Shikva nahi, shikva nahi, shikva nahi
Tere bina zindagi bhi lekin, zindagi, to nahi,
Zindagi nahi, zindagi nahi, zindagi nahi

Tum jo keh do to aaj ki raat, chaand doobega nahi, raat ko,
rok lo... (2)
Raat ki baat hai, aur zindagi, baaki to nahi

Tere bina zindagi se koi, shikva, to nahi,
Shikva nahi, shikva nahi, shikva nahi
Tere bina zindagi bhi lekin, zindagi, to nahi,
Zindagi nahi, zindagi nahi, zindagi nahi

(4)

Aarti man maanti
Kehna kyun nahi maanti
Paathshaalaa me chhutti ho gai
Bastaa kyun nahi baandhti
Bastaa kyun nahi baandhti
Bastaa kyun nahi baandhti

Aa … Aa … Aa…
Salaam kijiye aaye hain
Haan … Aa … Aa…
Salaam kijiye aaye hain Aarti devi

Aa … Aa … Aa…
Ye thekedaar hai bhaarat ki bhaarati devi

Salaam kijiye, aali janaab aaye hain
Salaam kijiye, aali janaab aaye hain
Ye paanch saalon kaa dene hisaab aaye hain
Salaam kijiye, aali janaab aaye hain
Ye paanch saalon kaa dene hisaab aaye hain
Salaam kijiye, aali janaab aaye hain

THE SONGS

O salaam kijiye
O salaam kijiye
O salaam kijiye
Aali janaab aaye hain

Jo in khudaao ko sajdaa kare naa qaafir hai
Bas ek vote *nahi hai ye jaan haazir hai*
O ... O ... Bahut lagaaye utaare hai naam ke label
Chalaai kursiyaan humne jamaaye hai table
Aa ... Aa ... Aa...
Hisaab dijiye hisaab dijiye hum behisaab aaye hain
Aa ... Aa ... Aa...
Hisaab dijiye hum behisaab aaye hain

Toh mil kar salaam kijiye aali janaab aaye hain
Ye paanch saalon kaa dene hisaab aaye hain
Salaam kijiye aali janaab aaye hain

Humaare vote *kharidenge humko ann de kar*
Ye nange jism chupa dete hai qafan de kar
Aa ye jaadugar hain ye chutki me kaam karte hain
Ye bhukh pyaas ko baaton se ram karate hain

Aa ... Aa ... Aa...
Humaare haal pe
Humaare haal pe likhne kitaab aaye hain
Humaare haal pe likhne kitaab aaye hain

Are bhai isliye
Salaam kijiye, aali janaab aaye hain
Salaam kijiye, aali janaab aaye hain
Ye paanch saalon kaa dene hisaab aaye hain
Salaam kijiye, aali janaab aaye hain

Ye paanch saalon kaa dene hisaab aaye hai aaye hai aaye hain
Salaam kijiye, aali janaab aaye hain

Humaari zindagi apni hai aap ki to nahi
Ye zindagi hai garibi ki paap ki to nahi
Aa ye vote denge magar
Ab ke yun nahi denge
Chunaav aane do
Hum aapse nipat lenge

Haan ... Aa ... Aa ... Ke pahale dekh lein
Ke pahale dekh le kyaa inqalaab laaye hain
Ke pahale dekh le kyaa inqalaab laaye hain
Ye inqalaab laaye hai haan

Salaam kijiye, aali janaab aaye hain
Salaam kijiye, aali janaab aaye hain
Ye paanch saalon ka dene hisaab aaye hain
Salaam kijiye, aali janaab aaye hain

THE SONGS

Aa salaam kijiye
O salaam kijiye
O salaam kijiye
Aali janaab aaye hain
Ye paanch saalon kaa dene hisaab aaye hain aaye hain aaye hain
Salaam kijiye, aali janaab aaye hain.

Appendix II

The Interview

ञ

Saba: Gulzar saab, let us begin with the beginning...

Gulzar: Yes. There is one thing that we should put on record – and that is – How did *Aandhi* get going? There is a little misconception about the whole thing inspite of the fact that it has been cleared in Kamleshwarji's lifetime itself. Kamleshwarji and I were friends. I used to write and he published them in *Sarika*[44]. We had published Meenaji's[45] diaries too. We used to meet quite frequently – Om Shiv Puri, Bhushanji – we were common friends. So, one day he asked if I was willing to direct, and in which case, he

---

44 A Hindi magazine.
45 The reference is to the popular actress, Meena Kumari.

had a story. A producer from the south wanted to do it. I told him that it would be my privilege to direct his story, and decided to work out the screenplay. He soon arranged a meeting with one Mallik Arjun Rao whom we used to call Malli sahib. He was the producer. Mallik Arjun Rao was obliged to Kamleshwarji because when Kamleshwarji was working for the Censor Board, there was a movie *Qeemat*, by Mallik Arjun Rao, which he had cleared. So, he naturally wanted to pay back Kamleshwarji, whom he considered to be a very dear friend. We went along with Kamleshwarji, and Bhushanji also came with us. Then we ran into a predicament. It used to be called Madras in those days, not Chennai. The predicament was that Malli sahib had a friend, philosopher and guide who had produced a film by the name of *Farz*, the one with Jitendra. He was like a moral guide for him. Only if he liked the movie's story, only then it was to be produced – this was Malli sahib's only requisite, and not a big hurdle. But it turns out that he didn't like the story which Kamleshwarji narrated to him, even though it was a very beautiful story. Set in a hotel, it depicted a cross-section of the society. The various kinds of people who come and go, and it could be very interesting. Since this person didn't like it, we got stuck in an awkward stalemate. There were some stories which he had in mind that he suggested a remake. 'Some Madras film could be remade', etc.

So Bhushan had an idea, just an idea which was, I think inspired from a novel by A.J. Cronin. That idea clicked. He immediately said that it was the kind of subject he was looking for, and it was the story we could do. There was a bit of embarrassment, but Bhushan was a very devoted friend. He said that the story had to be developed and that they could develop the story into a film together, and we decided to do it.

At the time, I was writing *Aandhi* and I intended to go to Mahabalipuram and complete my script. All of us went off to Mahabalipuram, but we ended up developing a story which was eventually released as *Mausam*. We agreed that we would first develop that story, and that I would continue working on *Aandhi* on my own.

I would write *Aandhi* during the day, and it became the topic of discussion during the evening. We felt as if both stories had begun to sort of intermingle and we asked Kamleshwarji to write a novel on both the stories. I was writing the screenplay. It was then called *Aagami Ateet*. I was the one to propose this kind of a title and he wrote a novel on both the stories.

When we returned and I had a fixed deadline, I had to narrate it to Suchitra Sen after about three to four weeks' time. As much as I am a person who runs away from work, I am also enthusiastic about what I get to work on. Neither Bhushan nor Kamleshwarji did their work and finally the three of us set out to visit the main location in Bhopal. Then one day, I got fed up. One evening, when we were in Bhopal, I spoke up. 'Look,' I said — we had just had lunch – 'this isn't happening. It's not working. I never miss deadlines. So I don't like the way things are unfolding.' As soon as I left the lunch table, I asked one of the hotel staff, 'Can you get me a taxi? A long-distance taxi. I want to go to Delhi.' (The Indian Airlines staff was on strike at the time.) He said, 'Right now?' I said, 'Yes, right now.' And I told my companions, 'You two can continue with whatever you want to work on. I'm going to Delhi and that's final.' But they replied, 'What will we do here? We'll also leave.' I quickly packed my things. I used to wear a lungi in those days and I got in the car, just like that, with the lungi on. I threw in my luggage … I was so irritated. I headed towards to Delhi, Kamleshwarji went to Allahabad and Bhushan left for Bombay.

I dumped myself in Akbar Hotel and told myself, 'I'll go out only when I complete my script.' There was a staff member there who worked tirelessly and took great care of me, day and night. I think he used to be around for twenty-four hours. I can't forget him. His name was JK and I named the hero after him. 'I'll name the hero after you, JK,' I told him. So, I finished my script and went away to Calcutta and soon the script was approved by the producer J. Om Prakash, Suchitraji and eventually everything was finalized.

Saba: Apparently there was this confusion that the story was written by Kamleshwarji but the script was written by you…

Gulzar: I told Kamleshwarji, 'It is up to you. I'll give you the title credit on the story. Go ahead and publish the novels based on your story.' Eventually, a time came when even the shooting of the film was about to be wrapped up. He finished writing it in a hurry and named his novel *Kali Aandhi* because the name *Aandhi* we had already taken for the film, so he wanted to establish the connection between the two. I even have a copy of the book which says, 'Your story dedicated to you.'

So this is how things were. Film is a medium in which changes happen all the time, sequences are changed … it happens a lot. So Kamleshwarji had once even complained to Bhushan: 'Bhai says one thing and makes something else!' He would call me 'bhai' and I would call him 'bhai sahib', that is all. And then in a hurry he wrote *Aagami Ateet* also. I told him that *Aagami Ateet* was entirely his and he could do as he pleased, but I won't depend on that at all. So, that's how I wrote both the scripts on my own and based on those he wrote his novels.

But there should be no misunderstanding here — this was a mutual arrangement, and it happens among writers. Say, I write a poem and he writes a story on it, or he writes a story on which I write a poem. It's all in good faith. It is only the outside world that could interpret this as something disgraceful.

Kamleshwarji wanted me to continue working along with him apart from doing only Malli sahib's story *Mausam*. 'Let's do it for *Aandhi* also,' he told me. So I told

J. Om Prakash that we'll be working together. Kamleshwarji was a well-established name – how could I refuse? So, this is how *Aandhi* happened and at the time it was not Indira Gandhi's life story. But even today, there is no one like her, so she was the best persona to keep in mind. Accordingly, that was the reference one could offer to any actor – the way she used to walk, the way she used to descend a flight of stairs, the way she would come out of a helicopter. We used her traits in good taste – not because the character was based on her or her life. But then things happened – the opposition parties remarked that Aarti Devi's character is shown to consume alcohol, and some decided to connect the two unrelated personalities. Further, seeing the advertisements and posters for the film, more trouble ensued. But for me, she was only a reference for personality traits and mannerisms. I think Kamleshwarji only took the name of Tarkeshwari Sinha[46] to escape from a situation.

Saba: I read about the changes that were made later to the film. Tell us about the two scenes which were added.

Gulzar: Yes, after the Emergency.

Saba: One of the scenes was where the dialogue, 'She is a role model' had to be inserted...

---

46 One of the first female politicians of India.

Gulzar: They made us add that bit. They insisted. By then the movie was running in its twenty-third or twenty-fourth week.

Saba: By then everybody had already seen it.

Gulzar: And we got to know about this in Moscow. It was screened in the Moscow Film Festival. We got to know that the screening was going to be cancelled since the film had been banned in India. Sanjeev [Kumar] was also there with me. After we got back, J. Om Prakashji tried very hard to have the ban lifted. We were already in the twenty-fourth week, so we decided to modify two scenes.

Later, at another time when I went to Moscow, I met I.K. Gujral sahib. He was now the Ambassador. Gujral sahib told me that it was Sanjay [Gandhi] who had not taken the controversy well. Otherwise, there was no objection from the others. I remember my reply too, that it was just one of those things which happens in a democracy![47]

---

47 I.K. Gujral was the Minister of Information and Broadcasting at the time of Emergency (1975) and was later appointed as the Ambassador of India to the Soviet Union. See 'Ex-Prime Minister IK Gujral dies at 92', *The Tribune*, 1 December 2012, https://www.tribuneindia.com/2012/20121201/main1.htm, accessed on 17 December 2018.

Saba: The choice of actors, Gulzar saab. Why did you select Suchitra Sen?

Gulzar: There's a story behind her selection too. J. Om Prakash, the producer, had called me for a story, which he wanted me to direct. Written by Sachin Bhowmik, it was a thriller set in a hospital or something, and he said that we could cast Sanjeev and Suchitra, and Sanjeev was, in any case, very keen to work with her. So Sachin Bhowmik had written the story accordingly, keeping the two actors in mind. In that meeting, Sachin Bhowmik, Sanjeev and J. Om Prakash were all present. I didn't particularly like the story – it was ordinary, a typical *bambaiya* plot. So, I said that it wouldn't be right to call Suchitra Sen all the way to Bombay to hear that story. Why should she do such a film? The first person in that room to react to my comment was Sachin Bhowmik. He said, 'You are right, absolutely right. This is Bombay, you can call many actors from here, but if you call Suchitra Sen, the story has to be something different.' When he said this, everyone else in the room agreed.

Personally, I'd already been thinking about *Aandhi* for quite sometime, so I decided it was the right time to narrate the story to everyone in the room. So I told them what I had in mind – two characters and their relationship, how it gets broken, she becomes a politician and we didn't have movies on politicians at the time, and viewers had not seen actual politics, how it worked behind the scenes.

I narrated just the basic plot and they all reacted positively. So J. Om Prakash said, 'Do you have this story on paper? Can you write it?' I asked for some time, and promised to share a synopsis in about two–three weeks. 'If you like it, then we can work it out,' I said. And he said, I will meet Suchitra Sen by the end of next month, or a month and a half or two months, or whatever. All this happened in that span of two months. As promised, I brought the synopsis in around two weeks' time because I already had the basic premise in my mind, not the entire story, so I began working on it. And that's how Suchitra Sen and Sanjeev Kumar came together to work in a film. So, filmmaking is full of many processes. It doesn't happen that the story is just sitting there for you and things fall into place and we begin casting and shooting. It's more complex than that. There are many questions: Who will play this role? When will we do this bit? There are hundreds of things which happen in making a film and it's a big team which works together.

Saba: And everything develops side by side…

Gulzar: Later I published the screenplay also. Kamleshwarji had no objection to it – among friends, among writers these things happen. Bhushan for example, was another selfless man – he never bothered.

It is not far from the truth to say that the problem with most film critics, reviewers and writers is that they have never made a film or been part of the making process, so they don't know how a film is made. Hundreds of things happen. An entire song is recorded and can later get cancelled! A male character is changed into a female character! So many things happen!

Saba: Tell us something about Sanjeevji, please. We know your equation with him – he is there in nearly all your films.

Gulzar: I knew Sanjeev – whom we called 'Hari bhai' – from the time he used to do theatre. I was in IPTA and he was in INT[48]. So, we met quite frequently at the Bholabhai Institute, Bombay and the two of us got along very well. We would perform together as well. He acted in Arthur Miller's *All My Sons* where P.D. Shenoy was the director. He played the role of a father at the age of twenty-three or twenty-two and Leela Chitnis played his wife. Manavendra Chitnis, Leelaji's son, was playing the son.

I had seen him play the role of an old man and he did a great job. It once happened that Papaji[49] had come and we all had stepped out to see him off. He asked Sanjeev once

---

48   Indian National Theatre
49   The reference is to Prithviraj Kapoor.

he had gotten rid of his make-up: 'That old man performed very well. Who was he?' That was a great compliment!

I knew that Sanjeev could play the role of an old man. For me, he was always the right fit for any kind of role – young or old. I've had two such anchors in the film industry – Sanjeev and R.D. Burman Sir. Unless the producer thought otherwise, these were the two people who would do anything for me. But the first film in which we worked together was *Sangharsh* and his scene with Dilip sahib[50] was the first shoot which I attended. I was a writer in *Sangharsh*. Although I was a great fan of Dilip sahib, I was thrilled to see that Sanjeev performed so well. It was Hari's scene all the way. 'Spectacular job!' I said. I was thrilled that my friend had done it. For anybody, even for Hari, it was an honour to work with Dilip sahib – before the scene and after the shot he touched Dilip sahib's feet and showed his respect for him. Moreover, even Dilip sahib appreciated him. Hari was a great associate, a great friend.

Saba: All of Sanjeevji's work is great, but in *Aandhi*, his performance is beyond his natural self. It's very difficult to write on that film because now, I watch that film every morning. One gets carried away by his performance. It is

---

50 The reference is to Dilip Kumar.

just perfect – the way he sits down, gets up, the way he speaks.

Gulzar: Two renowned actors are in that film – Suchitra and Hari. Suchitra meets him after a long time, notices him and says, 'You haven't changed!'. 'Gotten weak,' he says. 'Not weak,' she says. 'Thinner.' I mean their eyes are playing, looking at each other, yet shying away from each other. They are avoiding each other, looking the other way and remarking.

Saba: And she is looking all over the house and says, 'This place is really clean.'

Gulzar: 'Is there another woman in this house?' That's the question at the back of her mind.

Saba: Yes, it is unsaid but it's very apparent that she wants to know.

Gulzar: It is unsaid but it's there in the script. In the script I've written it. In the script those instructions are given to the actor that a doubt should be apparent. And then, looking for Mannu, she wants to know if there is anybody else. I think there were enough moments for me to provide both actors, and knowing their stature I knew how to go about it.

Saba: And to lead them ...

Gulzar: Yes. I mean that is what it is, what an actor needs. They are great actors but they need material to act and I think there was enough for me to provide to them.

Saba: There was more than enough. Tell us a bit about the songs, Gulzar saab...

Gulzar: '*Tere bina zindagi se koi shikva to nahi*' was the ideal song for the film. Both knew that it is their story being told and they could react to it. She takes his coat off and puts it away – that is such a lovely moment to start the music on. I had to create those moments to own the night.

Mattan is the name of that place, it is in Kashmir, on the way to Pahalgam. Gauri Prasanna was a celebrated Bengali songwriter. At the time, Pancham used to compose special songs during Durga Puja – in Bengal, it is a very big festival; new books are launched, new magazines released and new songs and albums are released. (To come out with a puja album once a year used to be a big thing.) So, Gauri *da* was working on a song for Durga Puja when I arrived with Pancham, who was working on a tune in Bangla. I was listening to him and ended up asking him if I could work on that tune. Pancham was surprised as it was a Puja song. I asked Gauri *da* also and he also did not have a problem.

Pancham on the other hand, was relieved! 'Now, I won't have to work on the tune at least!' – was his reaction. So, that is how '*Tere bina zindagi se koi shikva to nahi*' was set to tune.

Saba: But I have a big confusion regarding this song – what exactly did you mean with this line? The interpretation is a bit ambiguous.

Gulzar: No, it's a pun on the word.

Saba: Yes, I mean it's a big pun and that is the reason that in my book *I Swallowed the Moon*, I did not quote this song since I just could not translate it.

Gulzar: If I say, 'No other complaint I've got beside you in life…'

Saba: … It's got two possible meanings, right?

Gulzar: But without you what is life worth anyway? It's a way of saying, it's a compliment. '*Tere bina zindagi se aur koi shikva nahi*' except that you are not there. No complaint to life I have except that you yourself are not there, isn't that a compliment? And a great expression of love? Without you I have no complaint regarding my life except that you are not a part of it. And without you what is life anyway?

This is what it is. If you are not with me then that is all I can complain of. I'll share a couplet, '*Kisi ke jaane par humko koi gila to nahi/Bade qareeb se uth kar chala gaya koi*' (I have no objection if someone leaves/Someone sitting really close walked away). Doesn't it hurt? There is objection in it, right? So, you did complain, but what did you say? I'll recite another couplet '*Ghairon se kaha tumne, ghairon se suna tumne/Kuch humse kaha hota to kuch humse suna hota*' (You spoke to others and they spoke back/Had you spoken to me, you would have heard from me). One verse, two ideas, said in two different ways.

Saba: And ended up saying a lot of things.

Gulzar: Yes, so that's ... that's the beauty of this – *Tere bina zindagi se shikva to nahi,* but without you, life is not life, is it?

Saba: But it is very heavy. It is something very heavy in very simple words.

Gulzar: Yes, that is why. This is its characteristic. There are a lot of couplets, a lot of them ... can't recall them now, got some other on my mind.

Saba: In all the three romantic songs, I've tried to analyse the metaphor of travelling. Travelling appears in all three

– turns, roads, these kinds of elements. So, I've linked the three songs and they are three different stages of life and there is a chapter in this book on the songwriting of the film where I've stated that the relationship has also travelled. So, when you write, do you consciously link the songs?

Gulzar: It's all a process, a mental process. The analysis comes later. Instinctively, I assign the behaviour; when I say they were avoiding each other, avoiding looking at each other, and with a sigh she says that he has become weak but she isn't looking at him. So, when I'm writing this, I haven't analysed why she is avoiding him or that this character should look the other way and that their eyes shouldn't meet. If I'm imagining it, I'm running along with the process – the characters and their growth. Whenever I write a screenplay, from the very onset it is this process that runs alongside the writing process – *don't mention it now, we'll make it a point later when we reveal it*. So, it is not that everything is planned. The story has to grow, the screenplay has to grow, and that growth happens only if you know the stages mentally. Then it happens … on its own.

Saba: But when you start a film, do you have something in mind – say, the film should be on certain lines. For example, all your films are largely about relationships.

Gulzar: Yes.

Saba: This is the best example of a film on relationships.

Gulzar: Yes.

Saba: The rest of the politics – it's a backdrop and a commentary of sorts, but it's about the meeting and then the separation and then the meeting again. So, when you start writing, do you also have the end product in mind?

Gulzar: One has the graph of the entire story. Then when one starts narrating it – each person has his own style – in my case, there are a lot of flashbacks because for me, it's about the economy of time management that I go only to the dramatic moment, narrate it and return instead of narrating it from the beginning. I feel that the flashback is a more dramatic – and more effective – way of narrating instead of taking a story from the beginning. So, I try to pick up from a core or from a place in such a way that the entire story comes to light and that is an individual choice made by every writer. There can't be a law or formula about it – that is why each one has a different kind of narration.

Another example – When I wrote *Masoom*, I started the film with the entry of a puppy at a home. And there is a shot of the kids with the puppy and they hide it. Papa warns that Mummy won't like it. Now, how will Mummy react to it? And how to have 'Papa convince her, please papa' because he is so sweet. Come to think of it, I've narrated the entire story of *Masoom* in that one scene – I've defined the characters, I've defined the reactions to the third entry, of the child, what will happen when it enters – if the same thing happens but I've narrated the whole story with a puppy in one scene if you look at it. It's a very clever way of telling you what's coming – sometimes you want to say, sometimes you don't but after you've seen the film for the second time, you will recognize and be aware of what's going to happen. So, each time with every story there is a different way of narration. Right? I don't know whether you consciously knew it or not but come to think of it, now I realize what I've done. It's not a puppy for the sake of a puppy, there is a lot added to it, there is a lot more in it.

In *Aandhi*, when she finally confesses in front of the opposition party on stage by saying, 'You are defaming me … let me introduce you to my husband. He is my husband. You should have asked me, I would have explained.' To that audience, the people who were sitting there, for whom the whole episode is a scandal, she reveals all the details, that too publicly, she says, 'He is my husband and we have a child. The years that I should have spent with him, with my child, I've given them to you.' She changed the entire conversation and seemed truthful when doing so. But was she truthful? Or was she, as a politician, deploying a trick? So, that's the duality and that's the beauty of her character. Without it, where is the drama? There are layers upon layers – first, there is a straightforward interpretation,

111

that she was truthful and people turned in her favour, but at the same time there is another layer for analysis, whether she had been honest. Or did she play politics because she knew what it entailed. So, without saying anything specific, each one can make his or her own judgement about her character, and that is the beauty of any good story. The fact that new meanings can emerge when you peel off the layers.

A man needs to be given a contradiction so that he can prove a point. The truth only makes sense when you have proven wrong something that you believe is wrong. That is the only way to prove the truth. The husband who says, 'You are a wife, stay in your place, who are you working for? I don't know because this house doesn't need your money. For whom you're earning is your business.' He is not thinking of her status, he is too conservative, traditional. So, as a viewer, you'll appreciate a change in his character and his positives only when you've seen his regressive side. Hence, JK's closing lines: 'No ... I don't want to see you defeated. Go finish your work. I'll bring our child to you' creates an emotional moment. So, unless one says, 'Why is he saying this?' you will not be able to solve its contradictions. If there is no contradiction, there is no drama in the character. If from the very onset 'he used to believe in her' then that is not life. Life is how you come out of a contradiction and prove a point. I mean, he might have been brought up in a traditional manner ...

maybe his problem was that she was giving more of her time to the father than she was giving to her own house. It is a complex life and it's a complex character. There wouldn't have been much of a story if one was loyal and the other was not. That is the reason of '*Badi wafa se nibhai tumne humare thodi si bewafai*' (Very loyally you have played with my little disloyalty). You appreciate the layers. As you peel through those layers you find him saying, 'No, I don't want to see you defeated.' I think there can't be a bigger expression of love.

You enjoy something only when you've created a contradiction. That is how you create drama and storytelling is drama telling.

Saba: These two characters have shades of grey…

Gulzar: They are lovely characters. To wake someone up by dipping his hand in piping hot tea, it is very cruel!

Saba: 'Is the sugar to taste?'

Gulzar: 'Is the sugar to taste?' You can't call it cruel. It's very intimate. To use logic there – but the tea was hot, so his finger got scorched – then you are reading algebra, you are not reading life.

Saba: And then you are not reading poetry.

Gulzar: Yes, it's got a lot of layers. Another thing peculiar to *Aandhi* is that in the entire film – I don't know whether you realized it – there is only one female character.

Saba: Yes, yes … not even another junior female artist.

Gulzar: Look at any cinema, any film which has got a female and not one more female character in the film, yet it's (the whole thing) is so well balanced. It happens nowhere.

Saba: And it's a feminist film.

Gulzar: And it's a feminist film.

Saba: I've noticed that. Not even a junior artist in the background.

Gulzar: I mean there is not even a mother or a sister or a daughter. I don't think even the daughter has been shown on screen.

Saba: Right. There is just a short scene from the childhood…

Gulzar: That had to be shown because of the censor … it had to be added later … otherwise it's not there. But it's the quality of the script, the screenplay in the entire film – there is an orchestration of the characters, right? Let's add someone here, let's add a mother here, a father there, distribute things – with one female and I've carried the entire film on it with all males around and it's a feminist film. That's the beauty of the craft which of course one can only analyse and see, otherwise it's not so obvious. And if it were obvious, it wouldn't be fun.

Saba: Something about the qawwali, Gulzar saab? Is this the first qawwali that you wrote?

Gulzar: I don't remember if I've written any before. I don't remember that but it was meant to be a street qawwali and meant to be a political qawwali.

Saba: It follows the perimeter of a qawwali very well that the first two lines don't show up later ... but largely qawwalis are romantic.

Gulzar: Yes, but other than the form, the main thing was the political comment it made. I've tried that from the beginning for my first film, *Mere Apne* also; '*Haal chaal theek hai...*' (I am fine...). It was a political comment which I wanted to make and it was effective too.

Saba: It's very effective and these days it's even more effective with the elections in the background. Recently there was a qawwali in *Dedh Ishqiya*.

Gulzar: Yes, right. In its climax.

Saba: But I couldn't find any more qawwali. Have you written any more?

Gulzar: Umm … I don't remember.

Saba: I didn't find any.

Gulzar: About this film, I wanted to do away with a notion – here it's always the vamp who drinks, it's always the bad person who smokes. None of these are true, in fact, both presumptions are just ridiculous. So, I decided to do away with any scenes depicting the heroine smoking or enjoying a drink. There's only one shot where she is seen writing and I've shown a cigarette on her table. That scene was exploited by propagandists who drew parallels with Indira Gandhi. In another scene, JK hits his leg against a glass kept near her feet. It is such a polite way of suggesting, 'So what? Even in your career sometimes you have to make a drink and keep it there even if you are not drinking.' We take so much time in coming out of traditions. So, I thought why not break a few traditions in our films also. I tried. Nothing wrong if you get one smoke; why not? Like, say, a live-in relationship – it was there in society but cinema had not used it. In *Ijaazat*, there is a live-in relationship which is pure, pious and everything is right.

Saba: The beauty of *Ijaazat* is that the other woman is not a wicked woman, she is as beautiful as a wife.

Gulzar: They are … all three are positive characters and each one is trying to bring comfort to the other two. It is its beauty that all three are positive characters.

Saba: There was a connection between *Aandhi* and *Hu Tu Tu* also. Just like it seems *Maachis* is a kind of a sequel to *Mere Apne*, *Hu Tu Tu* looks like it is a sequel to *Aandhi*.

Gulzar: True. I agree with you. It is indeed like an update. That's what I say when people talk about remakes. A remake is not the same story once again, with tweaks to the characters' professions or costumes. You must update – the boys from *Mere Apne*, who fight with cycle chains and hockey sticks, now carry guns. The politician was using them there also and the politician is using them here also. The youth is dealing with the world around them. So it's fresh, but updated – that's the way to make a remake.

Saba: When you make a film, you have all the roles – writing, screenplay, director…

Gulzar: I pass through every character, their emotions, their tragedies, joys, everything … and I am the one who suffers the most. I used to do my readings myself to all the actors because I experience everything. I know what is happening to each character emotionally and that tells me or teaches me communication – is it communicating or not, because the word written for a film or on a screenplay or in a scenario, in a scene is ... not just a word. One has to understand the way it has been said and the weight that it carries with it, the emotion which is soaked in it. And the line means nothing if it does not carry that emotion. That's why the dialogue which I write helps in the growth of a scene, or of the relationship. Words have no meaning if they are not carrying an emotion with them, a purpose or a tone with them. That's very important.

I can tell you a few examples from different films. A character like Anand[51] can't sit idle – he must talk, he must do something, as he has to live the rest of his life within that period which he knows. But you can't measure his reactions; he has to be that instinctive. When he enters the hospital, a man walks by him and he says, '*Motey*', and nothing else. He cannot control himself – he has to say something – '*Ae motey*' (Oye fatty) and runs away. It has got nothing to do with the theme of the story but it's an instinct of the character. I had a little fear that maybe Hrishi *da*[52] would edit it, seeing it as an extra shot for no reason, but he appreciated it. He said that it was going well with the character.

---

51 The protagonist from the film, *Anand* (1973).
52 The filmmaker, Hrishikesh Mukherjee.

So, one has to travel with the character. For instance, in *Aashirwad*, I again had the fear if Hrishi *da* would keep or reject a particular scene. He was like another teacher for us – we kept on learning from him without even getting an idea ... So there is this one scene in a park, where a number of activities are going on simultaneously. There is a person who is reading the newspaper, there is someone who is playing, there is another person who is eating, and then there is a little girl in the park whose chain is snatched. Someone screams, 'chain snatcher' and the people gather around the little girl. After they have gathered, there are comments '*Dekhiyeji din dahade ye hogaya*' (See, this has happened in broad daylight), '*ye kaise ho gaya yaar*' (How could this happen now), and the guy who has been resting till now says, gets up and says, '*Ye government nahi chal sakti*' (This government won't work), and goes away! Whether the government would work or not has got nothing to do with it but these are the moments which happen in life. Hrishi *da* appreciated it so much that I felt fulfilled. Everytime, it is not a thought-out graph. Spontaneity has to go like this.

Saba: And how can you make two or three films together – *Aandhi*, *Khushboo* and *Mausam*?

Gulzar: No, they were not two-three together. I always completed one film and only then began working on another. I never shot two films at a time.

Saba: But they were released simultaneously.

Gulzar: That has happened because a film's release often takes time and the dates differ. But *Mausam* and *Aandhi* share a coincidence. On the day of *Aandhi's* premier I was beginning the shooting for *Mausam*. Later on, when the time for *Mausam's* premier came, I was shooting for *Aandhi* again because of the censor and the changes that I had to make. Even today, I always say that on *Aandhi's* premier I was shooting *Mausam*, and on *Mausam's* premier I was shooting for *Aandhi*. But that's only overlapping because of that censor work not otherwise. *Koshish* and *Parichay*, they were released with a gap of hardly a week or two – one at Metro, the other at Liberty in Bombay. In one, Sanjeev Kumar plays the husband, in the other he plays Jaya's father. So, release timings could be unpredictable. But I always made only one film. There were never two films that released together – never.

Saba: Both *Aandhi* and *Mausam* were released in 1975. But 1975 was an amazing year for films – *Deewar, Sholay, Julie, Jai Santoshi Maa, Nishant, Aandhi, Mausam* all released that year. In this book, I have called 1975 a watershed year for Hindustani cinema. Thank you, Gulzar saab for the insightful interview.

Cast and Crew

Suchitra Sen as Aarti Devi
Sanjeev Kumar as JK
Rehman as K. Bose
Om Prakash as Lallu Laal
Om Shivpuri as Chandra Sen
Manmohan as Mr Agarwal
A.K. Hangal as Brinda Kaka

Story – Kamleshwar
Director of Photography – K. Vaikunth
Art Director – Ajit Banerjee
Audiography – Navin Zaveri
Editing – Waman Bhonsle and Gurudutt
Playback Singers – Lata Mangeshkar, Kishore Kumar, Mohd Rafi, Amit Kumar and Bhupendra
Music – R.D. Burman
Producer – J. Om Prakash
Screenplay, Dialogues, Lyrics and Direction – Gulzar

Bibliography

❧

Anantharaman, G. 2008. *Bollywood Melodies: A History of Hindi Film Song*. New Delhi: Penguin Books.

Arnheim, R. 1957. *Film as Art*. Berkeley and Los Angeles: University of California Press.

Bashir, S.M. 2013. *I Swallowed the Moon: The Poetry of Gulzar*. New Delhi: HarperCollins Publishers.

Bhatia, S. 2013. *Amar Akbar Anthony: Masala, Madness and Manmohan Desai*. New Delhi: HarperCollins Publishers.

Bhattacharjee, A., and B. Vittal. 2011. *R.D. Burman: The Man, The Music*. New Delhi: HarperCollins Publishers.

CG, Manoj. 13 June 2015. 'SS Ray to Indira Gandhi six months before Emergency: Crack down, get law ready'. *The Indian Express*, http://indianexpress.com/article/india/india-others/six-months-before-emergency-s-s-ray-to-indira-gandhi-crack-down-get-law-ready/, accessed on 7 January 2016.

Chakravarty, S. 1993. *National Identity in Indian Popular Cinema 1947–87*. Austin: Austin University of Texas Press.

Chatterjee, P. 2012. 'Indian Cinema: Then and Now'. *India International Centre Quarterly*, Vol. 39, No. 2, pp. 45–53.

Chatterji, S. 2015. *Suchitra Sen: The Legend and the Enigma*. New Delhi: HarperCollins Publishers.

Chowdhury, M. 2013. *Uttam Kumar and Suchitra Sen: Bengali Cinema's First Couple*. New Delhi: OM Books International.

Desai, M. 2013. *Pakeezah: An Ode to a Bygone World*. New Delhi: HarperCollins Publishers.

Deshpande, A. 2007. 'Indian Cinema and Bourgeois State'. *Economic and Political Weekly*, Vol. 42, No. 5, pp. 99–101, 103.

Dhawan, M.L. 13 August 2000. 'He was an actor for all seasons'. *The Tribune*, http://www.tribuneindia.com/2000/20000813/spectrum/main3.htm, accessed on 13 January 2016.

Dutta, S. 2002. 'Globalisation and Representations of Women in Indian Cinema'. *Social Scientist*, Vol. 28, Nos 3/4, pp. 71–82.

Eleftheriotis, D., and Gary Needham (eds). 2006. *Asian Cinemas: A Reader & Guide*. Edinburgh: Edinburgh University Press.

Gulzar. 2005. *Pukhraj*. New Delhi: Rupa and Co.

Gulzar, M. 2004. *because he is …* New Delhi: Rupa and Co.

Kazmi, N. 1996. *Ire in the Soul: Bollywood's Angry Years*. New Delhi: HarperCollins Publishers.

Lal, V. 2011. *Deewaar: The Footpath, the City and the Angry Young Man*. New Delhi: HarperCollins Publishers.

Lockwood, D. 2016. *The Communist Party of India and the Indian Democracy*. New Delhi: Sage Publications India Pvt Ltd.

O'Donnell, Erin. 2014. 'Making Sense of Censorship: Censorium: Cinema and the Open Edge of Mass Publicity, by William Mazzarella'. *Senses of Cinema.* http://sensesofcinema.com/2014/book-reviews/making-sense-of-censorship-censorium-cinema-and-the-open-edge-of-mass-publicity-by-william-mazzarella/, accessed on 7 January 2016.

Pandian, A. 2011. 'Landscape of Expression: Effective Encounters in South Asian Cinema'. *Cinema Journal,* Vol. 51, No. 1, pp. 50–74.

Rajamani, I. 2012. 'Pictures, Emotions, Conceptual Change: Anger in Popular Hindi Cinema'. *Contribution to the History of Concepts,* Vol. 7, No. 2, pp. 52–77.

Ranade, A. 2006. *Hindi Film Song: Music Beyond Boundaries.* New Delhi and Chicago: Promilla & Co Publishers in association with Bibliophile South Asia.

Swarup, Harihar. N.d. 'Kamleshwar Brings Out the Truth of Life', http://www.tribuneindia.com/2003/20031228/edit.htm#3, accessed on 10 October 2013.

Zankar, A. 2013. *Mughal-e-Azam: Legend as an Epic.* New Delhi: HarperCollins Publishers.

Acknowledgements

❧

The idea of writing a book on *Aandhi* came about on the day I received the advance copy of *I Swallowed the Moon: The Poetry of Gulzar*. And the moment I shared the idea with Shantanu Ray Chaudhuri, then managing editor at HarperCollins India, he was as excited as I was. And, that is how I started work on this book.

I can never thank Gulzar saab enough. I got to know him when I was finishing my PhD thesis, which was a comparison of his film and non-film poetry (which later came out as a book, *I Swallowed the Moon*). I have been in touch with him ever since and got to know him as one of the most humble and affectionate persons around. He was always there for any query that I had during the writing process. His detailed interview in this book gives a unique insight into what went into the making of the film. Thank you very much, Gulzar saab.

Shantanu and I share the common bond of fondness for Gulzar saab's works, and in the last couple of years have spent hours mulling over them. Thank you, Shantanu and Harper Collins for trusting me with this book. I would also like to thank Arcopol Chaudhuri and Rinita Banerjee for the final edits of the book.

Thanks to Prasanna for sharing my excitement for writing and encouraging me to keep at it every time I would pause.

Ammi, Abbu: Thank you for always being there for me.

Amir and Sana, you have actually been there for me – physically and emotionally, through time, even when life was engulfed in one long *aandhi*. Thank you, both.

Thank you, God, for bringing these people into my life.